AN INSTRUCTOR'S GUIDE TO TEACHING MILITARY STUDENTS

AN INSTRUCTOR'S GUIDE TO TEACHING MILITARY STUDENTS

Simple Steps to Integrate the Military Learner into Your Classroom

Suzane L. Bricker

ROWMAN & LITTLEFIELD
Lanham • Boulder • New York • London

Published by Rowman & Littlefield
A wholly owned subsidiary of The Rowman & Littlefield Publishing Group, Inc.
4501 Forbes Boulevard, Suite 200, Lanham, Maryland 20706
www.rowman.com

Unit A, Whitacre Mews, 26-34 Stannary Street, London SE11 4AB

Copyright © 2017 by Suzane L. Bricker

All rights reserved. No part of this book may be reproduced in any form or by any electronic or mechanical means, including information storage and retrieval systems, without written permission from the publisher, except by a reviewer who may quote passages in a review.

British Library Cataloguing in Publication Information Available

Library of Congress Cataloging-in-Publication Data

Names: Bricker, Suzane L., author.
Title: An instructor's guide to teaching military students : simple steps to integrate the military learner into your classroom / Suzane L. Bricker.
Other titles: Simple steps to integrate the military learner into your classroom
Description: : Lanham, MD : Rowman & Littlefield, [2017] | Includes bibliographical references and index.
Identifiers: LCCN 2017012211 (print) | LCCN 2017014346 (ebook) | ISBN 9781475828450 (Electronic) | ISBN 9781475828436 (cloth : alk. paper) | ISBN 9781475828443 (pbk. : alk. paper)
Subjects: : LCSH: Soldiers--Education, Non-military--United States. | Soldiers--Education (Higher)--United States. | Veterans--Education (Higher)--United States. | Veterans--United States--Psychology. | Adult college students--United States. | Teacher-student relationships--United States.
Classification: LCC U716 (ebook) | LCC U716 .B74 2017 (print) | DDC 378.1/982835500973--dc23
LC record available at https://lccn.loc.gov/2017012211

∞ ™ The paper used in this publication meets the minimum requirements of American National Standard for Information Sciences—Permanence of Paper for Printed Library Materials, ANSI/NISO Z39.48-1992.

Printed in the United States of America

CONTENTS

Foreword	ix
Preface	xiii
Acknowledgments	xv
1 A Brief Introduction and Salute to the Military Student	1
1.1 Patterns of Instruction Based upon Tradition	2
1.2 Breaking with Tradition: Getting to Know the Military Learner	3
1.3 An Instructor's Friend: Basic Guidebook to Military Learners	6
1.4 Questions and Answers for Nontraditional Learners	13
1.5 Questions and Answers from Nontraditional Learners Who Are Military Students	17
1.6 Chapter Highlights	19
2 Why Should I Gear My Curriculum to Military Students?	21
2.1 Scenario: Experiencing Uncertainty	21
2.2 Are Military Students Prepared to Take College Classes?	23
2.3 Chapter Highlights	28
3 Constructing Syllabus Content	29
3.1 Scenario: Beyond Desperate Measures	29
3.2 Military Culture Defined	31
3.3 Comparisons between Academic and Military Genres	33
3.4 Setting Up Your Syllabus: Deadlines	36
3.5 Redefining the Socratic Method	39

3.6 Chapter Highlights	40
4 A Military Learner's Introduction to a College Campus: Directions on Resource Access	41
4.1 Why Is Acknowledgment So Important?	42
4.2 Charting the Right Path	42
4.3 A Campus Model for Providing Resource Access	43
4.4 Offering a Different Kind of Support	45
4.5 Tools to Advance Your Knowledge	47
4.6 What Does It Mean If Your School Has Been Designated as "Military Friendly?"	47
4.7 Useful Resources that Can Be Accessed Online	48
4.8 Resources Your Students Can Access on Their Own	49
5 Defining the Needs of Online Military Students	53
5.1 Using Technology to Transform History	53
5.2 Technology and Teaching: Keeping an Open Mind	55
5.3 From a Designer's Point of View	57
5.4 Knowing "Right" from "Wrong"	59
6 Who Is the Army Learner?	61
6.1 Who Joins This Branch of the Service and Why?	61
6.2 Goals in Pursuing an Education	66
6.3 A Question of Semantics	67
6.4 Factors Affecting Graduation Success	69
6.5 Success Rate in the Private Sector and Types of Careers Often Pursued	69
7 Who Is the Marine Learner?	71
7.1 Who Joins This Branch of the Service and Why?	71
8 Who Is the Navy Learner?	75
8.1 Who Joins This Branch of the Service and Why?	75
9 Who Is the Air Force Learner?	81
9.1 Who Joins This Branch of the Service and Why?	81
9.2 The Air Force from an "Academic" Perspective	84
10 Who Is the Coast Guard Learner?	87
10.1 Who Joins This Branch of the Service and Why?	87
11 Who Is the Veteran Learner?	91
11.1 What Defines This Category of Learner?	91
11.2 Our Role in the Classroom and Ability to Change Lives	93

	11.3 Factors Affecting Graduation Success Rates	94
	11.4 Following the Paper Trail	95
	11.5 Success Rates in the Private Sector and Types of Careers Often Pursued	96
12	**Who Are the Government Contractors, Reservists, and Military Family Member Learners?**	**99**
	12.1 Government Contractors: A Force unto Themselves	99
	12.2 Reservists: More than One Commitment	101
	12.3 Is Acknowledgment Important?	105
13	**Defining Basic Types of Medical, Physical, and Psychological Conditions that Can and Do Impact Military Learners**	**109**
	13.1 No Advice Is Being Offered	109
	13.2 The Trauma of Sexual Harassment	111
	13.3 Service-Related Injuries You May Not Be Able to Detect	112
	13.4 How Do These Conditions Affect School Performance?	112
	13.5 What Can You Do to Help?	113
	13.6 When Anger Is an Issue	114
	13.7 Adjusting to Physical Injuries	115
	13.8 A Veteran's Challenges	115
	13.9 How Much Are You Expected to Know?	118
14	**The Past, Present, and Future of Military Education: What the Experts Have to Say**	**123**
	14.1 Assessing the Best Approach to Providing Quality Education	123
	14.2 The State of Military Education Ten Years Ago	125
	14.3 The State of Military Education Today	129
	14.4 Prospects for the Future of Military Education	138
Selected References		143
Index		151
About the Author		155

FOREWORD

When World War II finally came to an end in 1945, some sixteen million service members, or about 11 percent of the entire U.S. population, returned home to parades and adulation as heroes. Yet, just beneath the surface of a rejoicing nation were serious questions regarding this massive transition of human beings back into civilian life. Would these veterans be able to find jobs? Would U.S. cities and towns be able to meet the sudden increases in demands for housing brought on by this mass transition of combat veterans back into society? For many of the transitioning service members themselves, the biggest question of all was "where do I go from here?"

These concerns were real. Unfortunately, the federal government had accumulated a rather bleak record when it came to providing for its veterans. Recall the events during the early years of the Great Depression, when veterans of World War I gathered in Washington, D.C., to demand immediate (though early) redemption of their service certificates awarded in the World War Adjusted Compensation Act of 1924. These "Bonus Marchers," many of whom had their families with them and had set up a sprawling campsite, had been out of work since the beginning of the Depression. The U.S. Army, under orders from President Herbert Hoover, ultimately drove them out and burned their campsite shelters and belongings. Yes, looking at the past record of governmental support for its military veterans, the expectation level for transition support for the World War II veterans couldn't have been very high in 1945. What's more, society had changed a great deal since the bombing of Pearl Harbor in 1941.

What kind of society, and more importantly, what kind of economy, were the World War II veterans returning to? In his outstanding book, *Over Here: How the G.I. Bill Transformed the American Dream*, Edward Humes points out that the U.S. economy had been revamped to manufacture military arms and equipment. Furthermore, women had entered the workforce in record numbers. Indeed, by taking jobs in the factories and shipyards across the country, U.S. women, epitomized by "Rosie the Riveter," enabled the men to enter military service and join the fight. It didn't take a genius to realize that significant government intervention would be needed, and that without it, the problems created by 11 percent of the population transitioning back into civilian life all at once would be much greater than anything previously experienced. However, there would be no veteran marches on Washington for the World War II generation of veterans, thanks to the Serviceman's Readjustment Act of 1944, or the *GI Bill of Rights*, as it is commonly called.

What the GI Bill did for our country was nothing short of phenomenal. Nearly eight million veterans took advantage of the GI Bill's education benefit. An entire generation of civic leaders at all levels received their education as a result of the GI Bill. The GI Bill's impact on the economy was equally impressive. The Congressional Research Service shows that the return on investment statistics are pretty impressive, pointing out that for every dollar spent on World War II GI Bill benefits, about seven dollars were returned to the U.S. economy. It is safe to say that an investment in the GI Bill was an investment in the United States.

Today's veterans are returning from what, for many, are multiple combat tours in Iraq and Afghanistan. Like the World War II generation, the current generation of veterans is returning to a U.S. economy that has been changed by the crash of 2008. However, although some 11 percent of Americans served in World War II, only 1 percent of Americans served in the Iraq and Afghanistan wars. Unlike the post–World War II years, today well-paying jobs with positive prospects for upward mobility are extremely competitive. These factors make the need for the attainment of a bachelor's degree from a top-quality college more important than ever. Although the GI Bill benefits are still available today in the form of the "post–9/11 GI Bill," many beneficiaries are unable to take full advantage and maximize the impact of the education benefit simply because the landscape of higher education has changed. Many veterans, having been disengaged from higher education for a number of years, lack confidence in their academic abilities. Others, older and more experienced than their traditional student peers, feel out of place culturally once they step onto a college campus. Still others are grappling with the additional responsibilities of families and children that inevitably take time away from academics.

Woefully, the Department of Defense (DOD) and Veterans Affairs (VA) do not offer in-depth programs to help veterans transition smoothly from the unique culture of military life to the vastly different culture of a college campus. Unfortunately, the so-called "civilian-military divide" referred to in the media is alive and well on college campuses and is all too often manifested in the student-veteran and professor relationship. The resulting de facto situation from the dearth of DOD/VA transition support is that the civilian-military divide for each student-veteran will, in most cases, either remain unchanged or will be mitigated based on the individual professors that interact with the individual student-veteran. This is why Suzane Bricker's comprehensive handbook is so important and, in my view, should be added to every professor's personal selection of pedagogical works.

College professors who are unfamiliar with military culture often rely on intuition when dealing with issues involving military and veteran students. In this handbook, Professor Bricker has painstakingly researched the issues that lead to barriers to success and has provided guidance for understanding and engaging not only the student–veteran, but also the active-duty military student and those students who are members of the military reserve component. She shows college instructors how to develop a better understanding of how to identify, integrate, and fully accommodate the learning interests and needs of military learners, leading to a better understanding of the unique challenges and responsibilities faced by this particular group of students. Through the application of the advice found in this handbook, the reader will come to better understand "military culture," the goals of military learners, and ways to tailor course-related content and incorporate methods for better communication with the various subsets of student-veterans and military learners.

As someone who has worked with hundreds of individuals transitioning from military service into higher education, this handbook—to my knowledge the only guide intended to inform those who teach military learners—is a welcome new resource.

Sidney T. Ellington, PhD, CDR USN-Retired | Executive Director
    Operation Opportunity Foundation | The Warrior-Scholar Project |
    From the Battlefield to the Classroom

PREFACE

> The mind is everything. What you think you become.
> –Buddha

To anyone who reads this book with the impression that I have a direct affiliation with the military, I do not. The truth is that I started this book with as much knowledge about the military as my anticipated readership.

Why then did I tackle such a difficult project? When I was hired as an online instructor by the University of Maryland University Colleges' (UMUC) Academic Writing Department, I began to notice something unusual about some of my students. E-mails would come in from deployed members of my class saying they could not access the Internet in time to complete their assignments, or from the spouse of a service member saying he would not be able to participate in a class discussion because his wife was returning home for a brief visit.

While I pride myself on trying to be fair to my students, the situations that were presenting themselves to me were unfamiliar. I began to wonder if other instructors felt the same way, and if someone like me, who does not have a military background, could respond to the types of questions I was being asked by my military students.

Nor could I find any resources to guide me toward a better understanding of where these students were coming from and what they expected of me. Therefore, my classroom became as much a forum of learning for me as it did for my students. I wanted to know these military learners so that I could ensure they were getting the same quality of education as their civilian classmates.

> Education is the most powerful tool you can use to change the world.
> —Nelson Mandela

Now it is time for you to take a similar journey of discovery that will help you to support military learners in your classroom. In this book, you will find clear and concise answers about how to assimilate military students into any classroom situation and how to address the frustrations you may have already experienced in locating resources to help you during this process.

Your goal, as the instructor, is to respond quickly and effectively to the unique situations that many of these students face as they work toward accomplishing the same goals as their civilian classmates. So, by using this text as your guide, you will first develop a well-balanced image of the challenges these students can face in trying to complete your class—challenges like having to ask you for a deadline extension because of immediate orders to deploy, or not being able to actively participate in your classroom discussions because of physical or psychological injuries sustained during active duty.

Thus, the pages of this book offer you practical suggestions on how to help your students locate on-campus resources for getting assistance with their classwork; accessing accommodations for physical, emotional, or psychological injuries related to their military service; or even paying their tuition costs through the post–9/11 GI Bill.

Finally, this handbook is a work in progress, because—as the last chapter indicates—we are facing an uphill learning curve to make sure that our own preconceived ideas about who military students are and what types of academic goals they are capable of achieving do not deter us from responding to their academic interests and needs. And if you are able to develop more meaningful interactions with your military students as a result of using this text, then the information has served its purpose. You can address these issues without compromising the standards of academic fairness and integrity you actively employ in your classroom.

> Each person must live their life as a model for others.
> —Rosa Parks

ACKNOWLEDGMENTS

I dedicate this book to my father, who served in three branches of the U.S. Armed Forces and was able to become a Nobel Prize–nominated nephrologist via this route. Although he passed away during the writing of this text, he was probably one of the few individuals who was impressed with my ability to write a book—even before I had completed the first chapter. Moreover, my stepmother, Ruth, who is my teacher, mentor, psychologist, spiritual advisor, and best friend all rolled into one, actually took the time to edit each chapter of this text as well as to tell me honestly when the message of my writing was unclear.

Furthermore, I could not have completed this project without my ongoing relationship with UMUC, which began when I was hired by Andy Cavanaugh, director of the Academic Writing Department. Some time later, I learned the value of networking from my direct supervisor, Mary Crowley, collegiate associate professor and course chair for the Communication Studies and Journalism Department at UMUC. She introduced me, via online interactions, to someone who put an important piece of the puzzle into place regarding students' rights and instructional privileges.

I also want to acknowledge the support I received from Lyn Ferguson, executive assistant to the provost at Harvard University. She recognized the importance of the message I am trying to transmit almost immediately and, therefore, enabled me to obtain valuable input from individuals affiliated with that institution.

Of course, this book could not have been written without the assistance of Dr. Sid Ellington, who took valuable time from his hectic schedule to discuss a cause he not only believes in, but also makes sure his goals for military learners come to fruition. He kindly agreed to write the foreword for this book.

Wick Sloane was one of the first people I interviewed, and reminded me how a person of integrity and humanity can still make a difference in this world.

A special thanks to Steven D. Westerfeld, communications specialist for the Department of Veterans Affairs for the Office of the Undersecretary for Benefits. He put the human touch on the interviewing process and made my outreach to high-level government officials become a realistic opportunity.

And without the support of certain individuals in my life, I am not sure I would have stayed on course throughout the drafting of this text. Thus, thank you to my kind and equally brilliant houseguests, Dr. Min Song and his wonderfully sweet and sensitive son, for making my life just a little bit less complex.

Finally, I want to acknowledge my nephew, Max, about whom I wrote my first published poem, and whose heart reminds me of the decency in this world.

I

A BRIEF INTRODUCTION AND SALUTE TO THE MILITARY STUDENT

For most college and university instructors, the first day of school can be nerve-wracking. Once the classroom door opens to an on-ground setting, or access is available in an online platform, you begin to ask yourself questions such as:

- "Am I prepared for a new term?"
- "Do I have enough lecture material and assignments to cover my subject matter?"
- "Are my skills contemporary enough to successfully engage this new group of students?"

Regardless of whether you have been teaching for many years or have just received your first assignment, you have a brief moment in time to establish a solid working relationship with your students. Initially, you will want to convince them that you are knowledgeable in your field to gain their respect. But having that knowledge does not guarantee you can motivate your students to learn.

Getting to know your students will show them you are interested in helping them achieve their goals and in creating a comfortable learning environment for them. To establish open lines of communication, you first want them to introduce themselves and explain what they hope to accomplish as a result of their participation in your class. Then, briefly share information about yourself and your own professional background.

Additionally, providing them with your contact information lets them know they can approach you outside of class for answers to specific questions about course assignments, class discussions, or lecture materials (Dreon, 2013).

1.1 PATTERNS OF INSTRUCTION BASED UPON TRADITION

In your classroom, you will generally encounter two types of learners: "traditional" and "nontraditional" students. "Traditional learners" are mostly:

- twenty-five and younger;
- recent high school graduates;
- single;
- living at home; and
- still receiving financial help from a parent or other family member. (National Center for Education Statistics [NCES], 2016)

Some traditional students, who are "returning learners" are familiar with the basic structure and function of a college environment. They are also more motivated to succeed this time around because they could be facing circumstances such as impending layoffs, retirements, divorces, or "empty nest syndrome" (NCES, 2016).

But not all students fit under the formulaic umbrella of a traditional learner. In fact, a growing number of your students may be "nontraditional learners," who are usually defined as follows:

- older than the traditional learner;
- more mature, with prior experience in making critical decisions;
- intensely focused on earning their degrees in four years or less; and
- taking a full course load, often while working to support a family.

Graduate students are typically female and enjoy the flexibility of taking their courses online (NCES, 2016).

1.2 BREAKING WITH TRADITION: GETTING TO KNOW THE MILITARY LEARNER

Teaching techniques that are applicable to the traditional learner may not apply to the military student. So, the first step is to understand what differentiates the military student from these more traditional learners.

> Do what you can, with what you have, where you are.
> –Theodore Roosevelt

Military learners are generally included among the ranks of nontraditional students who are frequently enrolling in both online or ground classes. They do not represent any particular social or economic class, but they do share common experiences. Unlike a traditional college student, who may be living at home and not have acquired practical experience in a real workforce environment, the military student's life is highly structured and dictated by a tightly compacted schedule that provides little room for flexibility in terms of time commitments.

For instance, look at the average daily military duties assigned to Lt. Col. Terry Thiem, PhD, strategic planner for the Office of the Assistant to the Chairman of the Joint Chiefs of Staff for Nation Guard and Reserve Matters–Pentagon.

Typical Deployed Schedule
0415–0430: Wake up, get dressed for PT
0430–0545: PT at gym
0545–0630: Shower, shave, get in uniform
0640: Catch van to work location
0700–0730: Log on, check e-mail, get briefed on any significant events
0730–0815: Walk to dining facility for breakfast
0815–1200: Work at desk / Attend meetings
1200–1245: Walk to dining facility for lunch
1245–1315: Talk to wife on Skype
1315–1400: Work at desk / Attend meetings
1400–1500: Go to flight line check on maintenance of aircraft/equipment

> 1500–1530: Phone conversation with program manager
> 1530–1730: Work at desk / Attend meetings
> 1730–1815: Walk to dining facility for dinner
> 1815–2100: Work at desk (possible DAU online course)
> 2100–2130: Catch van back to billet
> 2130–2200: Get ready for bed
> 2200–0415: Sleep (if there are no rocket attacks)
>
> —Lt. Col. Terry Thiem, 2016

Service members' professional backgrounds tend to set them apart from civilian classmates because they have learned to juggle the responsibilities of combat duty while continuing to provide financial support for their families. Or, they could be awaiting orders to deploy and exist in somewhat of a "holding pattern" during training activities.

These military learners may have also experienced frustrations in trying to secure their tuition funds through the post–9/11 GI Bill. Similarly for those on leave or who have left the service permanently; they can be stressed out by trying to find a job and a place to live, while working to reestablish meaningful relationships with their families and friends.

> Our goals can only be reached through a vehicle of a plan, in which we must fervently believe, and upon which we must vigorously act. There is no other route to success.
> –Pablo Picasso

Military students' goals are actually similar to the more traditional students' goals. They hope to:

- do well in class,
- learn skills that will improve their academic performance and workforce potential,
- be acknowledged for meeting the course objectives, and
- achieve a good grade at the end of the term.

But because the stressors of being deployed can be accentuated by a forced and prolonged separation from family and friends, the service member may have a negative emotional reaction to receiving a less-than-satisfactory grade from you or other instructors.

Colby Buzzell, who served as a government-trained trigger puller in the Army's Stryker Brigade Combat Team during the Iraq War from 2003 to 2004 and authored *My War: Killing Time in Iraq* and *Lost in America: A Dead End Journey*, offered the following observations about his classroom experiences to readers of a U.S. Department of Veterans Affairs blog:

> Academics have never been my strong suit. My final high school transcript has me rank at number 332 out of 344 students, which is nothing to brag about. But one of the many things I learned while serving in the Infantry are the phrases; "I can't" and, "I'm not good enough," or "I can't do it" don't exist. Especially while under fire (Buzzell, 2011).

One reason that good grades are so important to military students is that the outcome of their positive performance can lead to a promotion, helping them climb to the next step of a "well-defined hierarchy" that is common to the military (VA Campus Toolbook, 2012).

According to Daniel P. Fanella, PhD, instructional systems specialist for the U.S. Army War College's Department of Distance Education, military students are usually young adults who have higher motivation than their civilian counterparts, and want to know the benefit of being taught a certain subject matter. Moreover, their time is usually limited, so they do not want to be assigned tasks that are nonproductive. They also want to feel like their opinions are valued and their level of professionalism is acknowledged; therefore, they anticipate the person who facilitates the learning environment will be knowledgeable in his or her subject matter (Fanella, 2016).

Moreover, their strengths include the ability to work independently and to guide themselves toward the completion of their academic goals. On the flip side, they may not appear as adaptive to sudden or unexpected curriculum changes, and will consequently feel more comfortable when goals are clearly defined and instructional elements are "detailed and well-articulated" (Fanella, 2016).

But when military students walk into your classroom and see unfamiliar faces, they may feel extremely vulnerable as well (Barnes, 2015). If they are veteran learners, they could also be coping with physical, emotional, or psychological issues that have resulted from combat experiences.

While your responsibility is to guide them toward a common learning objective, if you have no direct knowledge about "military culture," you run the risk of marking down grades or failing them for the wrong reasons (National Conference of State Legislatures, 2014).

For instance, you may misinterpret why they appear uncomfortable when asked questions. You may also not understand why they seem reluctant to speak about their military experiences with classmates (Starr-Glass, 2013). In turn, if you place expectations upon them that they are unable to reach, you could accidentally give them the impression that you are unconcerned about their welfare ("Students Lack Interest or Motivation," n.d.). And, if they feel unsupported by you or by their classmates, they may lose interest in learning or stop going to classes altogether (Lighthall, n.d.).

Instructions on how to resolve such concerns are provided in this text, along with anecdotal information that will help you to interpret the needs of these military students.

1.3 AN INSTRUCTOR'S FRIEND: BASIC GUIDEBOOK TO MILITARY LEARNERS

This handbook is designed to provide instructors with the foundation they need to fully integrate military students into both online and on-ground classrooms to promote optimal learning. For instructors who may find it difficult to understand the depth and range of these students' experiences and the impact of those experiences on their classroom performances (Lighthall, n.d.), each chapter focuses on a different issue that you may encounter (Starr-Glass, 2013). Step-by-step instructions on how to resolve such concerns are provided as well, along with anecdotal information that has been contributed by military students themselves.

1.3.1 The Challenge of Gearing Information toward the "Nontraditional" Student: A Brief Introduction and Salute

As of 2013, one million veterans and their families used their post–9/11 GI Bill educational benefits to attend colleges, universities, or trade schools (National Conference of State Legislatures, 2014). That figure is more than 50 percent higher than U.S. Department of Defense estimates

A BRIEF INTRODUCTION AND SALUTE TO THE MILITARY STUDENT

that 325,000 serivce members signed up for similar classes in 2011 (Callahan & Jarrat, 2014). With enrollment figures increasing at such a rapid pace, you are probably feeling the pressure to make sure these students' learning needs are met. Yet, first, you must have a clear concept of who your military students are and how their experiences may set them apart from their civilian classmates. For purposes of this text, a military learner is defined as the following:

- someone who has recently enlisted into any branch of the U.S. Armed Forces;
- a service member who is currently deployed;
- a veteran, reservist, or U.S. National Guard member;
- a U.S. Department of Defense contractor; or
- spouses of active-duty personnel or veterans.

The military offers a unique environment to its service members. They are provided with food, medical care, occupational training, and recreational activities on a regular basis. So, when military learners become separated from this "cocoon-like environment" and have to learn how to navigate a college campus, they can feel like this new landscape is as foreign to them as an uncharted battle zone. As a result, military students may not appear very confident when they first walk into your classroom. You may also sense that they try to isolate themselves from peers and to disengage during regular classroom discussions. In truth, this attitude may reflect the fact that they feel like outcasts, particularly, if their academic advisor or campus officials have not reached out to them directly to make them feel welcome.

Joe P. enlisted when he was seventeen. So, after he completed his service and returned to college, he did not feel a dramatic age difference between himself and most of his classmates. But he could not understand why they constantly focused on trivial concerns such as asking their parents for permission to go to a party or late-night concert.

He began to withdraw from conversations with his peers. "I was not trying to prove that I was better than them," Joe said, "but I was definitely more mature."

Joe did want to get a good grade, so he tried really hard to participate in class during the first few weeks. But he began to contribute less during certain discussions that focused on the negative impacts of recent U.S. military actions. Joe's classmates knew that he had been in the military, so he started to feel like he was targeted by their anger.

"People would just stare at me, and I would feel uncomfortable," he said.

Joe quit volunteering information about his military experiences. Meanwhile, as the discussions about U.S. military operations continued, he became more withdrawn.

"Someone said in class, 'Well, they teach soldiers by sending them to school, so they can learn how to torture the enemy.'"

Joe realized that he really had no desire to challenge this student's opinions, since he was not taking this class to teach others or to change their minds. But the words stung nonetheless. "I felt like a monster, to be honest," Joe said, "realizing that people really thought that way."

Although he found comfort in vowing to never raise his hand in class again, Joe realized that he felt totally alone and, deep down inside, he felt very, very uncomfortable.

1.3.2 Remaining Aware in Classroom Situations

In the same way that Joe's classmates probably underestimated the impact their words were having on him, you may be totally unaware how your approach to teaching military students can, and frequently does, affect their learning outcomes. You may also misperceive why military learners appear unable to freely express their opinions in class or to ask for special accommodations for an injury, especially if the symptoms are not obvious (McBain, 2012).

Yet often military learners do have strong opinions, and may even be willing to voice them when they first walk into your classroom. But if they sense that you are trying to lead a discussion in a particular direction which is reflective of your own viewpoint, they may decide not to challenge you out of respect for your position of authority (Ellington, 2016).

In the military, they have been taught to follow rules that define limits on their freedom of speech (Martin, 2014). Hence, their lack of participation may be related to self-doubts about speaking freely and forming opinions that are based on their use of critical thinking skills. Perhaps that is why some veterans have stated that they would rather go back into combat situations than participate in classroom discussions (Mulrine, 2015).

Another problem that military students may encounter is that they have learned a technical writing style that is usually inconsistent with the requirements of most course assignments (National Conference of State Legislatures, 2014). Also, if they are suffering from post-traumatic stress disorder (PTSD) as a result of the environment(s) they were exposed to overseas, they could be dealing with mild to severe physical, emotional, or psychological symptoms as well (Elliott, Gonzalez, & Larsen, 2011). If they are currently deployed, they may not have frequent access to computers or their use of the Internet may be restricted in the global region where they have been deployed.

1.3.3 Accepting the Challenge

> Life is either a daring adventure or nothing at all.
> –Helen Keller

What steps can be taken to ensure your military students make a successful transition into the classroom environment and receive the same quality learning experiences as their peers? Your sensitivity to learners' needs is critical to helping them achieve their educational goals and objectives (Hayek, 2011).

Your greatest challenge then becomes finding the resources you need to translate a traditional pedagogical approach into teaching techniques which are more responsive to military learners' needs. However, according to an American Council on Education study of 690 postsecondary institutions, "only 47% offered faculty and staff any professional development training to deal with the military" (Starr-Glass, 2013). Additionally, you may not know how to direct your military students to resources they can access themselves if they feel unsupported during the educational process (VA Campus Toolbook, 2012).

Your ability to receive adequate training in teaching these military learners or to identify what campus resources are available to assist them, appears even more difficult if you work for one of the nation's top-rated universities. Such prestigious schools as Yale, Princeton, Washington University, Brown, Dartmouth, Duke, Johns Hopkins, Northwestern, Stanford, or the University of Chicago only admitted a combined total of 103 undergraduate veteran learners during 2015. And that number is actually decreasing, rather than increasing.

According to *Inside Higher Ed* columnist Wick Sloane (2015), such low numbers mean that veterans cannnot get the assistance they need to use their GI Bill benefits to offset tuition costs. Moreover, Sloane points out that the enrollment figures at some institutions represent a combination of veterans and their dependents (2015).

Terry Thiem acknowledges that many of the Ivy League schools do not have ROTC programs and that their attitudes may reflect a perception about the organizational features of a highly structured military environment. But he indicates that such impressions could be based on experiences from the past that may have "tainted their viewpoints" (Thiem, 2016). In fact, by not encouraging large populations of military students, they are missing out on a strong and talented field of applicants.

"I don't think it is an intelligence issue. I just think it is a cultural issue," Thiem says. "I could name probably a dozen top-level people with PhDs who are or were military members." In fact, Thiem himself joined the military to get educational benefits because his parents could not afford to send him to college, and he received the majority of his education, including his PhD, paid for by the military.

1.3.4 Eliminating Bias: The Pitfalls of Personal Opinions

> I've learned that people will forget what you said, people will forget what you did, but people will never forget how you made them feel.
> –Maya Angelou

If your institution does provide you with adequate training, then you have learned about such topics as:

- the distinguishing features of the military culture;
- the duties and missions of each service branch; and,

- the most up-to-date research on supporting the learning needs of military learners and their dependents (Saathoff-Wells, Dombro, Blaisure, Pereira, & MacDermid Wadsworth, 2016).

But knowing this type of basic information is not enough. You will still need to recognize how your own attitudes can, and often do, impact your students. For instance, if you or any of your students express antiwar sentiments during classroom discussions or ask military learners to voice negative opinions about a battle they have participated in, you may make them feel more isolated and withdrawn.

Generally, military students do not want to be asked to evaluate the ethics of civilian casualties generated during conflict situations. Veteran Alison Lighthall, who is a contributor to the *NEA Higher Education Journal*, states: "These [types of questions] do more than upset veterans; they wound the hearts of men and women who are already overburdened with sorrow" (Lighthall, n.d.).

Conversely, if you or their classmates praise military students and position them as national heroes during class discussions, they may feel just as overwhelmed (Zinger, 2010). So, in some instances, you may want to try and refrain from using common expressions such as "Thank you for your service to this country." You may not be aware that military learners think you are being apologetic to them for not understanding their circumstances, or that you are just trying to make yourself feel more comfortable being around them. Moreover, if you pose questions that require them to speak on behalf of their service unit or of the entire U.S. Armed Forces, you will probably be making them feel very apprehensive as well (VA Campus Toolbook, 2012)

One way to get to know military students is to create a proactive learning environment where they will feel more relaxed and willing to contribute. Since they are used to a very rigorous daily routine that divides their time up for them, you can establish a structure within your own classroom that will show them how much you value their time commitment (Flaherty, 2014).

You also do not want to position military learners as "victims," even if they have sustained serious injuries that you are notified of through their academic advisor. Expressing sympathy can actually have a profoundly negative impact on their motivation to succeed. The reason why this approach does not work is that military students were or are part of a large and complex organization that is focused on a singular mission. And to accomplish that mission, service members are instilled with the core values of strength, courage, and bravery.

This is the same mind-set that these students carry with them into your classroom. Because of the level of courage they have been asked to display during their service commitments, they may not be able to acknowledge, even to themselves, the extent or the nature of their injuries. So, if you try to address these issues with them, either in private or in front of the entire class, you may easily lose their trust. But if you focus on their abilities instead of their service injuries, you are more likely to help them achieve their academic goals (Lighthall, n.d.).

1.3.5 When You Become the One Who Is Being Observed

Keep in mind too, that military students will enter your classroom with their own preconceived ideas about how you are going to conduct the class.

- First, they are likely to assume that you have no military experience, and thus cannot relate to their professional backgrounds or experiences.
- Second, they are likely to perceive that your political views may be quite liberal, and that you could harbor some corresponding anti-military sentiment.
- Third, they may also believe that you are likely to show preferential treatment to classmates who have not served.
- Fourth, because you are a recognized authority figure, they expect that you will conduct the class in a highly structured manner that requires disciplined responses from your students. In that regard, you will severely discourage students from talking out of turn or from bringing such items as food or drinks into the classroom. When you set a deadline for group activities or written assignments, those deadlines will be strict and unbending.

1.3.6 How Can You Counteract Military Learners' Initial Impressions of You?

If you *do* have military experience, it is a good idea to share that information with them on the first day of class. You can also let them know if other professors or staff members at your academic institution have served and discussed their experiences with you. And, even if you are strongly opposed to the United States' involvement in any armed conflict overseas, you have a responsibility to these learners to make sure that you treat them with the same level of respect as their classmates.

Another way to gain military learners' respect is to prevent their peers from using cell phones during class and to demand close attention during your delivery of lecture material. You do not want to display any verbal or nonverbal communication that would compromise your position of authority in the classroom.

> Education is not preparation for life; education is life itself.
> –John Dewey

1.4 QUESTIONS AND ANSWERS FOR NONTRADITIONAL LEARNERS

More than likely, the majority of your students are going to be traditional learners. These students generally are unsure about how they are going to make the transition from high school to college or find their way back into an academic setting from a prolonged absence. So, you want to be prepared for their questions, which are usually related to how they can identify the most successful and direct route to obtaining their degrees. Some suggested responses are provided below.

- Question 1: What are your expectations for this course?

According to Chickering and Gamson (1987), "At various points during college, students need chances to reflect on what they have learned, what they still need to know, and how to assess themselves." So, when students are asking you what is expected of them, they are also trying to get a sense of who you are and how much effort they are going to have to devote to your class. Therefore, without going into too many specifics, you want to encourage them to pay close attention to your lectures, to come into class well prepared, and to frequently participate in corresponding discussions. Also, you want to reinforce that they are responsible for completing any and all reading and course assignments by their stated deadlines. Finally, let them know that they are responsible for monitoring their own progress and coming to you for feedback, if they have specific questions about any obstacles that could be impeding their progress over the length of the term.

- Question 2: Do you grade on participation, as well as on written assignments? Do you grade on the curve?

Depending on the guidelines your employer has set, and on your own decision about how to divide point values between each of the respective course activities, your response to students will differ. On the other hand, it is advisable to let students know that their participation is reflected in their final grade, so that you encourage cooperation from them and involvement in both class discussions and group assignments. Moreover, if you decide that an assignment was too challenging for most students to score well on, you may want to modify that content element and grade on the curve for the current semester.

- Question 3: Can students ask you for help if they are having difficulty completing their assignments? What is the best way to contact you?

Again, your response to these questions will depend on the policies of your employer. Moreover, your own participation will probably reflect your status as a full-time or part-time instructor. Because you want to encourage students by displaying an interest in their ability to work to their fullest potential, it is best to indicate whether you have regular office hours and can make an appointment to meet with them. If you are an online instructor, you can provide your e-mail address to them as well. Letting them know that you will respond within a specific period of time, such as twenty-four to forty-eight hours, will indicate your interest in their progress.

- Question 4: Do you have any recommendations about either online sources or texts that students can purchase to increase their chances of getting a decent grade in your class?

Generally, if you have been teaching for a while, you have periodically been asked to review sample books by publishing houses or have been given access to texts by your learning institution. If you have had a chance to access the online or on-ground library facilities associated with your school, you probably have a fairly good idea of what resources are available to assist your students.

Often, the teaching experiences you have will enable you to determine which sources to access. Look for reference material that is not only accurate, but also communicates ideas in a simple and clear manner. One particularly useful online source that provides quick and easy access to formatting information is titled *The Owl at Purdue*.

- Question 5: Are you a tough grader? If students want to get an A in your class, what basic steps do you recommend?

You do not owe it to your students to define yourself as either a "tough" or an "easy" grader. Let them form that opinion for themselves. What you can do is give them a general idea of what your expectations are for the course and what particular skills they will need to get an A.

Therefore, you can respond by saying your guidelines for A-level work are clearly defined in the syllabus, and then ask them if they have already reviewed that information. Also, when discussing these guidelines with them, provide a bit more detailed explanation in terms of one or more of the following:

Do you deduct points for late students?
Do you deduct points for late assignments?
How can a student contact you, if he or she is unable to come to class or has another type of emergency situation? Will you provide deadline extensions in such cases?
Do you allow revisions on any assignments?
Can quizzes be taken more than one time?
Do you spend time reviewing students' grades in class?
What is the best way to contact you and what times are you available?

Are you available to talk about specific problems that students have at any other time other than your regular office hours?

- Question 6: Some students haven't been in a college classroom in a long time. Do you have any tips about how they can be more successful this time around?

This is a question that you want to be prepared to answer, so carefully consider how you might respond, based on your experience with students who have faced similar situations. You can choose to use an anecdotal reference to help you explain your answer, but be sure not to include the name of the student whom you have based this story around. Your conversation could go something like this:

> Everyone in this classroom has the same goals, which are to do well and apply their credits toward getting their degree. So, one of the qualities that I stress is cooperation in group activities and course discussions. Your interest in the topic being discussed provides constructive feedback to your classmates too. Make sure that you are familiar with the due dates of class assignments and have completed the reading requirements before each class begins. Also, do not be afraid to ask questions or to voice your opinions in class discussions. I can only gauge your progress when I know what concepts you are struggling with and what topics you feel that you are able to easily grasp.

- Question 7: Do you think a student might have difficulty "fitting in" in your class because he or she is a returning student?

This is a touchy question, because your role in the classroom is to remain objective and not to show favoritism toward any specific individual. Therefore, when you provide an answer, consider letting students know you will evaluate their work in the same way that you do every other member of the class, but also tell them directly that you are glad they have decided to be in your class.

Continue to encourage students by recognizing the "small steps" they take to improve their participation in the class; "[r]ecognizing these small steps will help encourage shy students [to] continue to take positive risks and overcome obstacles" (Romano, n.d.).

1.5 QUESTIONS AND ANSWERS FROM NONTRADITIONAL LEARNERS WHO ARE MILITARY STUDENTS

If you have military learners in your classroom, you are encountering a unique subset of nontraditional learners. Remember that these individuals are likely to be older than their peers, shouldering a great deal of responsibility, and have probably had experiences that set them apart from their classmates as well as most of the general population.

Also, they may not know if they will adapt well to a classroom situation and could have many concerns about interacting with you and with their classmates on a regular basis. Moreover, a veteran learner is likely to be the first person in his or her family to attend college (VA Campus Toolbook, 2012). So, a list of potential questions that you could receive from such students, and sample approaches you can use to respond and engage the military learner, will follow.

- Question(s) 1: Have you taught any military learners before? Do you know anything about my background and experiences? How can I make a valuable contribution to this class, and do you think my military experiences will be an asset to my partication in course discussions?

Identify these learners as early as possible, and start to build credibility by asking them where they have traveled and facts about their military career that could make them feel more comfortable. Tell them honestly and directly if you have taught only a few military learners or encountered large numbers of these students in your previous teaching experiences. Learn and share as much knowledge about the military culture as you can.

- Question 2: Will you allow me to extend deadlines if my service commitments interfere with my classwork?

Tell military learners that you will allow them some flexibility in meeting deadlines, particularly if they are deployed, about to be deployed, or have sustained physical or emotional injuries during combat situations. Be sure to publish information in your syllabus that indicates what steps they should take to qualify for such extensions and include a brief encouraging comment to them about their ability to remain an active participant in your classroom.

- Question 3: Do my writing skills match your expectations? Can you help direct me to campus resources, if I need additional help to complete my assignments?

E-mail your direct supervisor before the term, or, if you have an admissions officer who is in charge of military learners, contact that person as well. Request updated information that you can provide to learners who may not be performing at the same level as their classmates.

Give these students honest and direct feedback, and ask them questions about how their writing experiences in the military differ from their course assignments. Provide a list of resources to students when the class begins and include on the syllabus specific actions you will take if students do not respond well to the basic writing requirements of their first academic assignment. Such a policy could state information like the following:

> Additional Information
> **** Please note. By the end of Week 1, you should be receiving written feedback on your work. If the instructor has indicated that significant or consistent syntax or grammatical errors are evident in your text, you are advised to contact your academic advisor for assistance or to similarly request additional guidance by e-mailing the (online or on-ground tutoring center).

- Question 4: Do you know how I can get help with making sure my tuition is paid by my post–9/11 benefits?

Be prepared with the name of the campus staff member who is in charge of military and veteran students and provide that person's contact information if requested. As a follow-up, ask students about their progress.

- Question 5: Are you aware that I need special accommodations because of an injury I received during my military service? Will you share that information with my classmates or anyone else on campus?

Let students know if you have received a letter from their academic advisor or from another school official. Be sure to thank them for their request, so that they feel more comfortable with approaching you about such a personal issue. Let them know that you are aware of their needs and that you can be contacted by e-mail or during your regular office hours if they want to discuss their situation.

Be sure your contact information also appears in the syllabus. Let them know how quickly you generally respond to requests from students, and reassure them that any personal information they give to you will not be shared with anyone else.

- Question 6: Are you going to ask me if I have served in the military in front of my classmates?

The best response is "no." Military students cannot be "typed" or "normed" by their decision to enlist, according to former Marine Sergeant Alexander McCoy, who recently published an Op-Ed piece in the *New York Times*. McCoy (2016) says that asking this question would likely produce one of two responses: 1) students might feel they have been put on the spot and believe they have no choice but to disclose their military status; or, 2) students might become extremely uncomfortable and try to deny that they have been in the service.

"I think it is important for instructors to try to set aside any stereotypes about what a military student is, and what situations they may have encountered," McCoy says. "I would compare posing that question to a current or former service member to asking everyone to identify if they are LGBT. It is not an appropriate question," he adds (McCoy, 2016).

1.6 CHAPTER HIGHLIGHTS

> The greater the obstacle, the more glory in overcoming it.
> –Molière

Adopting a New Approach to Teaching

For an instructor who has no idea what the phrase *military culture* means, this handbook identifies resources available to you so that you can improve the quality of the learning experience for your military students. The need for such a text is reinforced by the results of a 2012 survey conducted by the American Council on Education. These findings indicate that faculty and staff members need to show more "sensitivity to the unique issues faced by military and veteran students and their family members" (McBain, 2012).

According to academic researcher David Starr-Glass, "It is more effective and respectful to approach learners—whether they are military students or students of a differing culture—through a recognition and appreciation of their cultural difference" (Starr-Glass, 2013).

Moreover, with about one million service members expected to use their GI Bill benefits to transition back to the private sector between 2015 and 2020 (Mulrine, 2015), you are being asked to respond to these concerns more often. But McBain (2012) points out that "Part of becoming more responsive to military and veteran students is understanding their needs, as well as recognizing what campuses do and do not do well in serving them." As a result, you have to know how to fully integrate the military student into the classroom and to provide access to appropriate learning resources within your own institution.

2

WHY SHOULD I GEAR MY CURRICULUM TO MILITARY STUDENTS?

2.1 SCENARIO: EXPERIENCING UNCERTAINTY

Jack P. went into the military at the age of seventeen to find relief from perpetual boredom. His mom was an executive at a large Fortune 500 company, and his father was a successful corporate attorney. But Jack did not really get along with either one of his parents, and he also felt he did not know what to do with the rest of his life.

College was one option, but it was just too soon for him to make that decision. Moreover, Jack was from an affluent family but did not want to ask any of them to help finance his education.

Even though Jack did not know anyone who had been directly affected by the terrorist attacks on 9/11, he felt motivated to enlist. Yet, shortly after his first deployment, he entered a combat zone and accidentally set off an improvised explosive device (IED). The IED fragmented his skull, leaving tiny shards of shrapnel in several parts of his brain.

Jack was treated for his injuries and later diagnosed with a condition called, traumatic brain injury (TBI), for which he received an honorable discharge. The explosive device may have done physical damage, but it had not changed his desire to go to college. Knowing his military units would not transfer, he still wanted to try and get his undergraduate degree as quickly as possible.

Jack was accepted at a prestigious university close to his home and was asked to complete a form advising his instructor of issues he had with meeting assignment deadlines. Unfortunately, soon after the term began, he realized that he could not read a single assigned chapter of his textbook in less than four hours. He felt frustrated, knowing that the same task would have taken him only 45 minutes before his injuries. Jack decided to talk his teacher about the problems he was having. But her response was not what he had expected.

"Why have you enrolled at this university?" the professor asked Jack. Her silence let him know that the conversation had ended.

Jack had learned in the military not to talk back to authority figures. So he kept his reactions to himself. But six months later he dropped out of school, because in his mind he felt like he had faced a rejection far worse than the physical impacts of an explosive device.

2.1.1 Supporting the Team

Most online or on-ground classrooms are set up as team structures with a preselected number of students working individually, as well as in groups, to achieve a common goal. A team structure also promotes cooperation and mutual respect. According to a *ScienceDaily* article: "Good ideas are rarely created in a vacuum. They often emerge when people refine their ideas in response to suggestions and comments received from colleagues" (Washington University, 2012).

To sustain this level of cooperation in your own classroom, you want your students to be attentive, receptive, and responsive to the course material. However, you also hope they will use their critical thinking skills to absorb information faster and develop their writing skills more effectively (Lindholm, 2005). Ultimately, most students hope these skills will help them to obtain stable and higher-paying jobs (CollegeAtlas.org, 2015).

Military learners are used to working in team environments that require them to accept great levels of responsibility on a daily basis. Moreover, they view their fellow service members as "colleagues," which is

WHY SHOULD I GEAR MY CURRICULUM TO MILITARY STUDENTS?

how they tend to see their classmates too (Flaherty, 2014). You want to communicate a clear understanding of your course objectives to them because reinforcing basic principles such as completing their assignments on time and in a professional manner will help them to know your expectations and accept their roles.

2.2 ARE MILITARY STUDENTS PREPARED TO TAKE COLLEGE CLASSES?

You want to establish a clear and consistent channel of communication with your students as soon as possible. If not, the learning environment is not really conducive to an open and ongoing exchange of ideas, and all of your students can be impacted (Chickering & Gamson, 1987). Consider, too, that your students are consistently evaluating themselves in response to your feedback to determine how well they are absorbing the critical course content elements and be able to succeed in achieving the course objectives. They will also compare their personal career goals to the perceived practicality of skills they are learning in your class.

You want to explain to your students how their past experiences can help them relate to these learning concepts. Chickering and Gamson (1987) point out that your ability to respect "diverse talents and ways of learning" will enhance the educational experience for everyone involved. Moreover, some of the most updated information on military students is provided here to assist you in identifying who these students are and why some instructors share common misconceptions about their learning abilities.

2.2.1 The Nature of Myths and Erroneous Assumptions

Myths are commonly based on a true, basic underlying principle, but the stories themselves are purely fiction. Along these same lines, when you encounter military students for the first time, ask yourself: are you creating your curriculum based on assumptions that could be described as "myths"? The questions and corresponding explanations that follow will help you to determine your answers.

- Common Myth #1: Military students are not ready for college.

False. In reality, doubts about a military student's ability to succeed in a college environment are often generated by the learners themselves. For instance, individuals who decided to join the military because they felt comfortable in an academic environment can tend to question their qualifications for reentering a college or university as well. As a result, many military students do drop out of school, whereas others are met with low expectations on the part of university instructors and staff members who do not understand the military culture.

But the reality is that "the vast majority of these students are perfectly capable of completing their degrees" (Callahan & Jarrat, 2014). Their approach to learning is focused, goal-oriented, and mature. This attitude reflects their ability to cope with high levels of stress on a daily basis, maintain a well-disciplined and responsible response to conflict situations, and serve in a leadership role, as well as to respect authority (NASPA Research and Policy Institute in partnership with Inside Track, 2013).

- Common Myth #2: Military students cannot succeed in obtaining their degrees.

False again. Ability is not the main reason that these students sometimes face major challenges in obtaining college credits for their military training and experience. Some have trouble meeting state residency requirements. Veterans, in particular, have difficulty getting their training and experience to transfer into college credits. It is only recently that educational administrators and policymakers have begun to address these challenges by offering veterans immediate access to in-state tuition rates and support program (National Conference of State Legislatures, 2014).

- Common Myth #3: Military students have all received similar training and approach their education from the same perspective.

If you have not served in the military, you may tend to believe these students are quite similar in their approach to education. You may also act compassionately toward them or give them special consideration if you perceive the impact of their battle encuonters could be affecting their academic performances.

But U.S. Air Force veteran M. Borcyourt disagrees with this approach. You should not "feel sorry or apathetic towards us," he says, nor assume any information about the learner's academic potential. Instead, Borcyourt urges you to "Embrace the discipline and commitment that we (military students) have," by asking them questions about what service branch they are affiliated with as early in the term as possible. "We are no different from the rest of the students," Borcyourt adds, "We have a slightly different background, and our experiences shape us."

- Common Myth #4: Most military students drop out of college because they have physical or emotional issues that affect their ability to complete classwork.

False. According to the results of a recent study completed by the NASPA, these opinions are false as well because the problem does not really originate with the learners, but with the type of guidance that they receive.

"Student veterans come from a background of high standards and expectations, and this becomes a permanent part of their work ethic," author David Vacchi (2013) points out. "If they find students, staff, and especially faculty to be slacking, it can unbalance a veteran into taking action, voicing concerns, dropping a class, or worse, dropping out of school."

Even the idea that most military students have physical or mental problems that can prevent them from completing their coursework is invalid because only about 20 percent of veterans fit into this category. Moreover, those who do experience such issues are still frequently found on college and university enrollment rosters because their injuries do not necessarily render them incapable of completing their education (Vacchi, 2013).

- Common Myth #5: Military students do not need college educations because their training has prepared them for civilian jobs.

Not true. The military's mission is not to prepare its service members for jobs in the private sector. Even though it does provide training in fields such as health care, piloting, and communications, as well as in trades such as mechanics, welding, cooking, dentistry, and computer repair, these skills will probably need to be enhanced through other learning channels, such as in your classroom.

Thus, consider that veterans between the ages of twenty and twenty-four are twice as likely to be unemployed as civilians in the same age category (New York Civil Liberties Union, n.d.). The length of time a person stays in the service does not affect this statistic (Mixon, 2014).

Even if you memorize the names of miltiary learners who are on your roster, you may not know what to do to help improve those students' experiences or to accurately interpret how your attitude will impact their performance (NASPA Research and Policy Institute in partnership wtih Inside Track, 2013). Additionally, once a military student leaves your classroom, you have very little chance of tracking his or her future progress because most postsecondary institutions do not know why temporary or permanent leaves of absence are reported among this partular subset of learners.

- Common Myth #6: As the course instructor, you can develop a clear understanding of what your military students have experienced if you have received the proper training from your learning institution.

Education does not equate to experience. If you have never served and are not related to someone who has, you can develop knowledge about the "military culture," but not know what it is like to be deployed or to participate in combat situations. You will also have a difficult time understanding the organizational structure and policies of the military because its actions are not governed by civilian laws or court systems.

Additionally, the media can cast a "red herring" in your direction, by broadcasting images of enlistees constantly being berated by their supervisors or communicating the message that all service members carry guns with them everywhere they go. Yet, if you actively engage your military students during class discussions, and complete professional development workshops that describe "best practices" in terms of how to treat these learners, you will be better prepared to transfer this knowledge into your pedagogical approach.

- Common Myth #7: Military learners entered the service because they could not succeed academically, and therefore, had few other options.

Also untrue. Some people like to paint a broad brush stroke across cultures they know little about and consider to be different from their own, according to McCoy (2016). Unfortunately, this type of labeling can

WHY SHOULD I GEAR MY CURRICULUM TO MILITARY STUDENTS? 27

unconsciously occur when you first scan your roster and identify your military students, or when classmates learn their affiliations as well.

Men and women who enlist do so for numerous reasons. They could be:

- trying to earn money to offset their tuition costs,
- expressing their feelings of patriotism,
- believe in the mission of the military as an organization, or
- be attempting to determine what type of careers they want to pursue.

Others join for "pragmatic reasons," such as hoping to obtain access to U.S. citizenship, or a means of improving their financial future and their ability to "climb into the middle class." Still others enlist because it is a family tradition.

"And if you look at the states where large numbers of military service members come from," McCoy (2016) adds, "there is not a 'red state/blue state' divide."

That being said, "nearly 83 percent of military officers possessed a bachelor's degree or higher in 2010, compared with almost 30 percent of the general population. The same year, more than 93 percent of enlisted service members had a high school diploma or some college under their belt, compared with 60 percent of American civilians" (Hunter, 2014).

So military learners actually represent the same cross-sector of the population as their civilian counterparts. Moreover, their abilities vary, as do their motivations for entering the service. Consequently, their contributions to the classroom are more affected by the attitudes of people around them, rather than their own academic abilities.

- Common Myth #8: Everyone who joins the service is deployed and is usually stationed in some remote and isolated location. Their only access to a computer is inside of a makeshift tent or temporary barracks that have been set up.

Each member of the service is required to complete at least one tour of duty, which usually lasts about four years. During that time, they may or may not be deployed. If they are, they are usually sent to a base station in the United States or in another part of the world. These temporary living quarters can be aboard ship as well as on land. If they are ordered into combat, they leave the base, travel to the area where the conflict exists, and then return to the station once the situation is resolved or the fighting is temporarily halted.

While they are living on base, they are assigned a regular job. So, in a sense, they have to meet their supervisor's performance standards in the same way that a civilian employee would. But when they have free time, they can use one of the recreation centers on base to access their classroom. If they do not own a laptop, they can use the computer equipment that is provided. So the amount of time they have to complete coursework depends on how much free time they have.

2.3 CHAPTER HIGHLIGHTS

Attempting to identify the military learner by their service affiliation is a losing proposition. No one likes to be stereotyped, and some of the assumptions about these students appear to be influencing their enrollment numbers at the nation's top universities, as well as their ranks in most graduate and undergraduate schools.

But a military student is just that—a student. They want the same results as their peers, which are to earn good grades and to gain the skills they need to be more marketable in the civilian workforce. To try and pigeon-hole these individuals as "slow" or "unwilling" learners shows signs of disrespect for their determination to achieve their academic goals. Moreover, if you treat these students differently from their peers, you could be affecting their motivation and, ultimately, their performance in your classroom.

3

CONSTRUCTING SYLLABUS CONTENT

3.1 SCENARIO: BEYOND DESPERATE MEASURES

John G. woke up one day and found himself in a body bag. The former Army infantryman had been injured by an improvised explosive device (IED) and was presumed dead by the servicemen who had retrived his body from the wreckage. Once the military medical staff realized that John was still alive, they began immediate treatment and medevaced him three consecutive times, until he ended up at Walter Reed Army Medical Center in Bethesda, Maryland.

Unfortunateley for John, however, his left eye took a year to heal, and many of his other injuries were internal. But because he had always planned to complete his degree after his military service ended, he decided to pursue this option immediately after he had received a medical discharge.

John was offered a scholarship through a military assistance organization and therefore had the opportunity to attend one of the top undergarduate schools in the country. The struggle he was experiencing, however, was how to complete his courses and still keep his medical appointments at the VA clinic. If he scheduled classes on the wrong day and missed a single doctor's appointment, he could lose his post–9/11 GI medical benefits forever. But if he missed too many classes, he would lose his scholarship money.

Signing up for classes was only the first of many hurdles that John learned he would have to overcome. When he walked into class on the first day, he realized he was the only military student in the room. Initially, he would try to volunteer information about his military experiences during class discussions, but stopped abruptly after other students started to stare back at him in response. He was uncomfortable and felt completely alienated from his peers.

While he was in the military, John had made friends for life. He had served on patrol, where he sometimes had to sleep in or next to his vehicle or in a trench hole he had dug for himself, but he had never felt alone because everyone had worked together to achieve a common goal. Looking back on these experiences, John said, "You just don't make friends like that. They do not exist outside of that environment."

A few weeks into the term, John started to develop symptoms of an illness that he refused to admit that he had—posttraumatic stress disorder or PTSD. Although his physical injuries were slowly beginning to heal, John found that his ability to function in the classroom was diminishing. And as his own anxieties quickly increased, he felt as though he was being more harshly judged by his instructor as well as by his peers.

To make matters worse, class discussions often focused on conflict situations he either knew about or in which he had participated. When his classmates described their fierce opposition to the U.S. military's actions in Iraq and Afghanistan, they never considered that he had actually served and been severely wounded in such conflict regions.

"I felt like a monster, to be honest, that people really thought that way," John said. Over time, John's symptoms progressed, and he stopped attending many of his classes. When he forced himself to go after prolonged absences, his instructors either did not even notice his appearance or asked if he had been deployed again.

John stayed in his room for longer periods of time, and even though the military had taught him to remain strong, he wept for hours on end, uncontrollaby.

One day, during a class discussion, an instructor asked John, "Did you ever kill anyone?" Although the Army veteran had never formed judgments against people who chose not serve, he found that the biases directed toward him were overwhelming. He went into his counselor's office to request help and tried to contact his departmental dean, but was told that he did not deserve special recognition because many other students faced hard times as well.

John's tears turned to shame when he had to choose between finishing his classes with failing grades or dropping out of school entirely so that he did not lose his military benefits. He completed the term, but the school would not allow him to reenroll because of bad grades.

John's PTSD symptoms progressed even further, so that he no longer could go outside of his small apartment, and he developed a serious drinking problem in response. For now, at least, he is able to reassure himself that his military benefits are still intact.

3.2 MILITARY CULTURE DEFINED

Getting to know military learners does not mean enlisting. Instead, it may only require you to take an active interest in your students by identifying their unique range of skills and experiences. But if you have preconceived ideas about people who voluntarily enlist or harbor strong oppositional feelings toward the United States' involvement in certain global conflicts, such views could cloud your perceptions about who these military students really are.

In chapter 1, the phrase *military culture* was used to identify the behaviors and values that are common to students affiliated with any branch of the U.S. Armed Forces. This definition is being expanded in this chapter to help you construct a more military-friendly syllabus and basic course content.

3.2.1 Getting Down to the Brass Tacks

When people enlist, they sign a contract, swearing an oath of allegiance to place the welfare of the nation above their own. And once they begin basic training, they quickly become integrated into one of the most diverse organizational structures that exist, one which has made significant strides to include members of the LGBTQ community and to allow women to play principle roles in combat duty. They are also provided free meals, a roof over their heads, and health care, as well as long-term medical and financial benefits and vocational training.

"Poverty and the desire to get out of poverty can be a real motivator, says Dr. Sidney T. Ellington (2016), a retired Naval officer and executive director of Operation Opportunity Foundation—The Warrior-Scholar Project. But, he adds, "the goal of getting an education will not carry you through your commitment. If you do not have a desire to be in the service, you are probably not going to make it" (Ellington, 2016). Other factors that can prompt someone to enlist include a sense of patriotism, wanting to do something worthwhile, a chance to learn skills that could lead to more lucrative employment in the private sector, and ambitions to travel (Clayton, 2012).

> After a hard day of basic training, you could eat a rattlesnake.
> –Elvis Presley

During his training, a military recruit is taught to be strong and to make calm, rational, mature decisions. But these characteristics can actually serve to deter their progress in an academic environment. One of the reasons for such delays is that military student have learned not to ask for help because such actions can be viewed as a sign of weakness. So, rather than approach you or ask their peers for help in interpreting key course content elements, they may simply start to internalize beliefs that they do not have the skills or abilities to succeed.

Military students may also doubt their ability to effectively communicate their ideas in written assignments, particularly when asked to write longer research papers. These learners have been taught to communicate in a clear and direct manner, so that their supervisors do not have to spend time "decoding" their messages. They are also accustomed to using a technical writing style and not to seek credit for the originality of their own ideas.

The format and style of writing used in the military is quite different from the requirements of an academic paper. So when military learners review the course syllabus and see that they have a forty-page research assignment due within a matter of weeks, they could easily begin to panic or feel overwhelmed. Even though they have already assumed responsibilities that require a level of maturity their classmates may not possess, they may also feel like they have no real connection to an academic environment. Such feelings are greatly enhanced if a military student never took college-level courses before or during his or her enlistment.

When you make contact with your military students at the beginning of the term, get to know their backgrounds so you can develop a better sense of what to do in these types of situations. Moreover, tips on how to construct a "military-friendly curriculum" are provided in this chapter in a narrative format that compares how military students have been trained to write with what an instructor expects during the development of a research assignment.

3.3 COMPARISONS BETWEEN ACADEMIC AND MILITARY GENRES

Writing courses are required at most colleges and universities, and therefore may be among the first classes that military students take. Yet, the instructors who teach these courses are usually unaware what on-campus resources are available to assist the learners with their writing skills and have not received specific training in teaching military populations. Additionally, instructors do not generally have a list of accepted guidelines to refer to when they try to help military learners transfer their skills to an academic format (Flaherty, 2014).

The suggestions here are intended to create a foundation for establishing a set of standard guidelines and procedures you can implement in your own writing classes and use to help prepare your course assignments as well.

3.3.1 Recognizing Basic Differences

Understanding how a military correspondence is constructed can help you to become more sensitive to the concerns of your military students. For instance, each document is usually focused on delivering one key central message or idea. That message has to be directly correlated to the organization's overall mission, which is to defend the country, while minimizing a potential loss of lives. In addition, the purpose of constructing such documents is usually to communicate a message to an internal audience.

Therefore, the scope of readership is often intentionally restricted, particularly in the case of classified documents.

When you encounter military learners, you will probably need to explain to them that the basic objective of an academic paper is to encourage new ways of thinking about a specific topic of interest or importance. Moreover, encourage them to discuss the types of correspondences they have prepared for the military. They will probably tell you that they are used to writing memos, personal letters, position papers, or staff studies for a principle audience. They may also indicate that they have been taught to use an outline format and to construct single-page correspondences to enhance the reader's accessibility of related information.

And they could indicate that military correspondences are likely to contain very little detailed information or extensive use of descriptive modifiers, so that the contents of these documents can be read and absorbed quickly. So, you will probably have to introduce them to the basic format and structure of a research paper. You will also have to indicate that length requirements can extend up to thirty pages or more, and be sure to tell them that content elements such as "sub-headings," chapter titles, and graphic images serve basically the same function as bulleted points and PowerPoint slides, in terms of highlighting important information for the reader.

Military students may also point out that they have been asked to prepare documents using numerous acronyms, which include "DEROS" (Date Eligbile to Return from Overseas) and "AWOL" (Absent Without Leave). You will probably have to explain to them that jargon is not used frequently in most academic writing assignments, unless this technique element is included in a quote or source title.

Your students might also tell you that they were taught to follow the guidelines of a specific style guide to ensure their documents were constructed in a uniform style. For instance, the Air Force uses *The Tongue and Quill*, which identifies the correct format for oral, written, and online communications. You can let them know that academic papers adhere to specific structural and technique guidelines as well. And, if they need additional guidance in understanding how these two styles differ, refer them to scholarly texts or online sources that include examples of research papers and formatting techniques that they will need to know to correctly document their sources.

One resource that is particularly useful for online and on-ground learners is a scholarly web site, *The Owl at Purdue*. In simple and direct language, this site provides the student with explanations and examples of in-text and bibliographic references that are formatted using APA and MLA styles. Or you could choose to provide your students with a written handout that you have developed for the class as well.

3.3.2 Expanding Definitions of "Acceptable Practices" for Military Learners

By far the greatest challenge you will probably face is explaining to your military learners why the concept of plagiarism is unacceptable in an academic environment. "There is not plagiarism in the military," Ellington (2016) points out. "As long as I am taking language and ideas from another DOD publication, then no one expects me to cite that." In fact, the military student has been taught to write documents that contain input from multiple authors and not to give credit to any previous or future contributors.

So, you can review the school's plagiarism policy with them in your office, and ask them if they understand why the consequences of such actions can be so serious. You can also ask them if they know how to correctly document sources, and explain why this process is necessary when they write an academic paper.

Explain to them that a research paper requires the use of scholarly sources to support the credibility of their own ideas. Similarly, be sure to emphasize that their sources must be cited in their text and on the references page as well. As a rule of thumb, you can indicate that any words, phrases, or ideas that do not originate from their own thoughts or ideas will require citations. Moreover, you want to explain the purpose of electronic "fact-checking" software such as *Turnitin.com*, to let them know these resources are used to establish the "authenticity" of document content.

Comparing military and academic styles of writing clearly highlights several reasons that military students often have trouble adjusting to an academic environment. You play a critical role in helping these students understand that being strong does not mean they have to remain silent, they can come to you at any time if they have concerns. However, you also want to keep in mind that these learners may not have been in a classroom situation for many years. So, when you post your guidelines of accepted practices and behaviors in the classroom, be aware that the university's plagiarism policy may require the following expanded approach:

> If you are a military learner, I am aware that you are used to constructing documents that may have originated from another person. Moreover, you probably have not been required to give credit to the original author during the completion of your own work. Therefore, if you have specific questions about how to translate the writing guidelines and policies you have been taught in the military into the requirements for constructing an academic research paper, you are welcome to e-mail me via my faculty address. I will respond to your request within twenty-four to forty-eight hours.

If they describe their experiences to you about constructing military documents, serve in the role of an active listener. When they are done, you can ask them to create a small T-chart and to write down the basic elements of a military correspondence they have just described to you on one side. Then, review the basic guidelines and format for a research paper. Ask them to write down each of the rules you have described on the opposite side of the T-chart, across from the characteristic of a military correspondence that appears to be similar.

Once the list is completed, you can suggest that they review both sides of the T-chart and identify whether any of the items they have listed about academic writing appear to pose particular challenges to them. You can then suggest that you are available to offer them additional guidance during your office hours, or, if your college or university has a writing center, suggest that they request assistance from an available tutor. But be sure to let them know that you can provide them with additional feedback while they are completing an assignment.

3.4 SETTING UP YOUR SYLLABUS: DEADLINES

Discipline is an essential tool in achieving course objectives. Instructors use the syllabus to reinforce the rules and to create a "working contract" with students to clarify what actions must be taken to fulfill the class

CONSTRUCTING SYLLABUS CONTENT

requirements. Many instructors choose to read the syllabus out loud the first day of an on-ground class or post an announcement directing students to review that particular content element in a virtual platform. During the term, if students want clarifications of assignment instructions or due dates, you can also refer them to the course schedule, which is included with the syllabus.

3.4.1 Time's Up! What about an Extension?

Rules for extending deadlines are usually specific to the course instructor and also depend on the time length of the term. Embedded somewhere in these guidelines for late submission is usually the phrase "no exceptions," which indicates that these rules are both fixed and final.

However, when most instructors are considering how to compose their late policies, they are trying to find language that will reflect the impact of unexpected life circumstances, such as an illness, death in the family, job relocation, travel for business or pleasure, or financial hardship. One factor they may not consider is that their students could suddenly and unexpectedly disappear from the classroom because they have received immediate orders to deploy.

Once again, the concept of military culture must be considered during the preparation of the course syllabus. So, you can choose to highlight specific instructional elements that explain your requirements for receiving deadline extensions on specific assignments to service members who could be or are currently deployed. The following questions are meant to help you compose an updated late policy that reflects your consideration of these learners:

- What type of documentation will you require of military students that states they have been or are about to be deployed? Will this documentation be required in all cases?
- What channel of communication should students use to submit their documentation? Do you want that information e-mailed directly to your faculty address? What deadline will you impose for submission?
- Will you set a maximum time length for your deadline extensions? What consequences are there for the student if the document is not received by the stated date?

- Can military students request more than one deadline extension per term? Under what conditions? Will you allow any exceptions?
- What adjustments will you make during online or on-ground presentations to accommodate the needs of military learners with injuries and illnesses such as PTSD and traumatic brain injury?
- What options for assignment submission will you allow for a student who does not have computer access?

3.4.2 Reducing the Role of the "Reinforcer"

Instructors know that the guidelines they incorporate into the syllabus must be clear, so that students are aware of what is expected of them. On the other hand, the list of deadline restrictions and late-policy rules cannot be so severe that students feel discouraged from wanting to take the class.

When setting deadlines for military students, however, one additional factor has to be considered. Although these individuals start out with the same learning objectives as their classmates, they are often faced with environmental factors that can delay, interfere, or even prevent them from achieving their goals. For instance, consider the case of the following student, who is responsible for monitoring computers operations for a U.S. Air Force base installation in South Korea. Close to the deadline of an assignment, she sends you an unexpected e-mail, describing issues she is having because of working irregular hours to cover shifts for other people. Although she indicates to you that she is now back to her regular schedule, she also states that she needs more time to complete the assignment.

Situations like these are not that unusual when you have military students in your class. And although you know that you are required to enforce strict guidelines on meeting deadlines, you also have to factor in that military learners are facing unpredictable situations. Therefore, it is usually advisable to be a bit more flexible in your grading policies. For instance, you could add the following information to your course syllabus:

> My grading policy applies uniformly to every student. However, for those of you who are actively deployed or could receive orders to deploy in the near future, I understand that your professional commit-

ments could cause unexpected delays in submitting your assignments by the required deadlines. Therefore, I am willing to work with you as long as you are able to inform me of your circumstances by e-mail, and provide me with a brief description of the issues you are facing that could impact your class participation or performance.

Please know that each member of this class is grateful to you for your service to this country, and I think we all recognize that your level of commitment to your military duties can sometimes place you in situations over which you have no control.

3.5 REDEFINING THE SOCRATIC METHOD

Your primary role in the classroom is to guide your students toward a better understanding of the course content and lecture material. Over time and with experience, some instructors can forget that they need to remain flexible to accommodate the changing demographic of their student populations. By adopting a more flexible approach to developing your curriculum, you encourage an open dialogue with your military learners.

3.5.1 Scenario: Climbing to the Top the Hard Way

In a recent political discussion that took place in an Ivy League college classroom, the instructor launched into a description of U.S. military actions in Iraq and subsequent civilian causalities. Two students were present who had fought, served, and sustained injuries in that particular global conflict. Their names are Colleen and Jermaine. Colleen had been shot during her first time on the front lines, and Jermaine had helped to medivac his best friend out of that particular war zone after he had been severely wounded.

Because these two students had a great deal of firsthand information about the topic the instructor was discussing, they hoped to be able to offer their own unique contributions.

At least, at first. But as the instructor continued, his diatribe became a bit more vitriolic, and so the two students decided to remain silent.

"It was like he was saying to us, 'Let me show you how much smarter I am than you,'" Colleen said.

Over and over again, the instructor kept reinforcing his opinions about the United State's wrongful use of military force in Iraq. He never asked for input or different viewpoints from his students—nor did he consider that these two military learners were in his class.

The instructor finished his speech and felt a great deal of satisfaction that he had been able to convey his carefully conceived and well-researched ideas to his students. What he did not consider was that he had also just created an invisible barrier between himself and his military learners.

3.6 CHAPTER HIGHLIGHTS

Preparing the syllabus and course content materials will enable you to establish a basic direction for your class. Also, by setting deadlines, you are indicating to your students that certain conditions must be met for them to receive full credit for their work and participation in the classroom. But sometimes a tremendous gap exists between ideas that will work in a classroom and practical situations.

In some ways, the presence of military students will enable you to bridge that divide by developing an understanding of the real-life responsibilities these individuals have faced and how those factors affect their academic performance. Your interest in these learners can help you to devise a curriculum that encompasses the needs of every class member.

If you accept such a challenge, you will probably be viewed as a much more caring and compassionate educator, one who is capable of responding to the changing demographic of both graduate and undergraduate students.

4

A MILITARY LEARNER'S INTRODUCTION TO A COLLEGE CAMPUS: DIRECTIONS ON RESOURCE ACCESS

Tell me and I forget.
Teach me and I remember.
Involve me and I learn.
–Benjamin Franklin

Military learners are not all alike, and therefore, their responses to your teaching style will vary as well. Moreover, according to education writer Colleen Flaherty (2014), these students cannot really engage if they feel their instructors do not understand or relate to their experiences. So, when you encounter a military student for the first time, and that person asks you questions about how he or she can benefit from your instruction, what tools do you have at your disposal?

When you look for guidance in helping military students achieve a more interactive role in your classroom, the resources you will probably find contain either inaccurate or insufficient information. Because your main job is to educate these students—as well as to guide them toward the achievement of their learning objectives—serving in an advisory role carries responsibilities that are probably not written directly into your contract. Teaching is a profession that requires skill, patience, knowledge, and experience. So, the instructor has to focus his or her efforts on the needs and interests of military students.

4.1 WHY IS ACKNOWLEDGMENT SO IMPORTANT?

Education is not the filling of a pail, but the lighting of a fire.
–William Butler Yeats

An article that appeared on Teaching Excellence & Educational Innovation Students web site contains the following advice: "Students are not only intellectual but also social and emotional beings, and all these dimensions interact to impact learning and performance" ("Students Lack Interest or Motivation," (n.d.). The article states that "[n]ew knowledge cannot be built effectively on a weak foundation," and similarly that "[k]nowing how students conceive of knowledge and of the role of teacher and student in learning can be a helpful starting point for designing instruction ("Students Lack Interest or Motivation," (n.d.).

So your ability to teach military students requires you to recognize that they may, and probably will, pose questions you have never been asked by a traditional student. And you want to be able to provide answers that can help them to transfer their professional skills into an academic environment (Roost, 2014).

But teaching is not a static process that simply requires the delivery of lecture material. Equally essential to the successful outcome of any learning experience is the active participation of each student in class discussions, group activities, and peer evaluations. Students need to feel that learning is a collaborative effort and that their participation is essential. They must develop trust in you and your ability to provide them with a quality learning experience in order to remain motivated during the learning process.

4.2 CHARTING THE RIGHT PATH

Military students have the same basic expectations as their civilian counterparts. On the other hand, they look to you as someone who can establish discipline and structure in the classroom. They also expect you to provide them with clear and direct explanations of the course material. Yet McBain (2014) points out that "[p]art of becoming more responsive to military and veteran students is understanding their needs, as well as recognizing what campuses do and do not do well in serving them."

As a result, the instructor has to know how to fully integrate the military student into the classroom by providing access to appropriate learning resources within, and outside of, his or her own institution. But strategies that work well for traditional learners appear to have less impact on military students.

4.2.1 Establishing a Connection

Some instructors work for institutions that recognize the value of preparing their adjunct and full-time instructors for the rising influx of military learners. If you are fortunate enough to be hired at one these schools, you know that they offer you workshops, training seminars, and on-site personnel who can respond to your questions by phone or e-mail.

4.3 A CAMPUS MODEL FOR PROVIDING RESOURCE ACCESS

The University of Maryland University College (UMUC) has made it a priority to facilitate the needs of military students, veterans, and their families. UMUC's admissions counselors and advisors assist these learners with selecting their certificate or degree programs, planning their courses, going through the registration process, exploring military tuition assistance and veterans educational benefit options, and identifying how many of their credits will transfer toward their degree programs.

Some of these staff members work on military bases in the United States, and they meet on site with spouses or other family members, too. In addition, advisors can assist active-duty service members and veterans with securing accessibility accommodations, such as specialized computer equipment or modified seating to optimize their learning experiences. Moreover, peer support is offered through UMUC's Veterans Success Club, which is a charter of the Student Veterans of America.

Additionally, UMUC offers special tuition rates for active-duty service members, members of the National Guard and Reserves, and their dependents. UMUC makes additional tuition funds available to post–9/11 educational benefit recipients through the Yellow Ribbon Program and operates a call center 24/7, 365 days a year, to answer questions about financial aid options.

4.3.1 UMUC's Model Approach

James Cronin, vice president of UMUC's Stateside Military Operations, indicates that the University's unique training module for its staff and faculty members encourages a better understanding of how to work with service members, veterans, and their families.

"The key is communication," Cronin says. "Military students, like other students, are expected to meet the standards in the class, but we have procedures to help them. So, instructors need to listen, and try to guide the students in the right direction, if assistance is needed" (Cronin, 2016).

The retired U.S. Army Lieutenant Colonel indicates that UMUC encourages the hiring of active-duty service members or veterans for teaching positions and is always looking for new ways to improve its outreach and communications with military students. He also offered some tips for faculty members who may not have the same training opportunities that UMUC provides, which follow.

4.3.2 Directing Students to the Right Resources

- When you are hired for an adjunct or full-time position, try to find out which offices you can refer your military students to and what services they offer. For instance, does your university have military advisors? Or is the registrar's office the place to refer a student who is trying to get his or her tuition paid through the post–9/11 GI Bill?
- If you do get questions from your students that you cannot answer, ask for advice from your academic director or another administrator who is used to dealing with military learners.
- If a student tells you that he or she has orders to deploy, try using one or more of the following strategies:

  - Tell the student that you will provide a reasonable deadline extension on any assignments that are due during the period of

deployment. Also, make sure that the student contacts you just as soon as he or she has Internet access.
- Give the student the option of taking an "incomplete," if his or her deployment will severely affect his or her in-class performance or ability to complete coursework. But make sure to document the specific reason(s) that you have made this decision, and provide that information to both the student and to the registrar's office, or other university officials who are responsible for implementing grading policies.

- If a student asks you how to get a refund for classes that he or she cannot complete due to deployment, try to determine which on-campus office to refer his or her request. At UMUC, such concerns are called "military withdrawals," and the university works with an armed force services representative to evaluate each request.

4.3.3 Requesting Credit for Military Courses Completed

What if students ask you how they can get credit for training or courses they have completed in the military? UMUC has a Prior Learning Program that recruits faculty members to review students' written portfolios of their previous training and professional experiences.

Some universities use the portfolio review process to determine if the student's experiences have qualified for enough transferable credit. If the outcome is positive, then the student is able to receive college credits for work experiences, including his or her military training. The awarding of credits means that they can "opt out" of taking one or more graduate or undergraduate classes. Guidelines used during the review process are consistent with academic standards set by the American Council on Education (ACE). Ask your director if a similar program exists at your school or suggest that one can be implemented.

4.4 OFFERING A DIFFERENT KIND OF SUPPORT

Not all schools have the same size military population as UMUC, which enrolled more than 50,000 active-duty military, reservists, dependents, and veterans during fiscal year 2015 ("UMUC at a Glance," 2015).

Therefore, other institutions could place significantly less emphasis on serving this particular student population, and the instructors' access to resources could be limited as well.

However, most schools do seem to recognize that military learners' approaches often differ from their peers. In that regard, the University of Wisconsin–Stevens Point has established a pilot program geared specifically to veterans, which is headed by associate lecturer David Chrisinger.

4.4.1 Practicing a New Approach

Chrisinger runs the "Back from the Front: Transitioning from the Military to Civilian Life" course, which is designed to help veterans successfully reintegrate into the private sector. Students are required to research how veterans of previous wars made similar life adjustments and to discuss their findings with classmates. Chrisinger describes these sessions as similar to military debriefings. After Chrisinger provides students with his own comments, he then instructs them to chronicle their thoughts and ideas about their military experiences.

"If you get 'buy-in' right within the first five minutes," he says, "the class is going to go well. So I spell it out in black and white: here is what we are going to learn today; here is the main point; here is what it means" (Chrisinger, 2016).

Although Chrisinger is not a veteran himself, he has earned his students' trust through a unique pedagogical approach that he describes as "deductive reasoning." He says that students are willing to share their experiences if they feel they are in a supportive environment where they will receive honest and direct feedback. Many of these literary works now appear in a published anthology titled *See Me For Who I Am* (2016).

"The fundamental paradox of military service is that you get a lot, but you get a lot taken away," Chrisinger adds. "So, my goal is to help these students use their military skills—such as leadership, project management, and time management—to understand how they can succeed in an academic environment as well as in their future careers" (Chrisinger, 2016)

4.5 TOOLS TO ADVANCE YOUR KNOWLEDGE

If you want to increase your knowledge about how to better serve the military learner, the U.S. Department of Veterans Affairs web site has been developed for just that purpose. The "School Resources" homepage appears beneath the tab on the left-hand side, and is titled "Education and Training."

The strengths of this resource are its readability and an underlying empathetic approach to defining the needs of military students. Moreover, each section begins with a brief introduction of a significant topic that would "key in" the college instructor or administrator about a specific need or challenge these students can, or do already, face. Then, more detailed descriptions are offered of what services are available and URLs or other contact information are provided for easier access.

The site also offers a list of upcoming workshops you can attend around the country. But an even more beneficial link appears under the heading "Student Veteran Assistance," and is titled VA Campus Toolbook. Once you click on *What Can I Do To Help?*, you can access practical information about how to construct your syllabus, including a brief sample welcome to military students (VA Campus Toolbook, 2012). Other tips include how to set deadlines and where to refer students who are coping with issues related to their combat experiences.

The Campus Toolkit includes other useful handouts that can be accessed online in PDF which provides detailed explanations of each service branch and definitions of military ranks. A one-page fact sheet offers bulleted points on veteran learners, and can be printed out for future use as well (VA Campus Toolbook, 2012). Horton explained that the level of support a veteran receives can mean the difference between a "soft landing and a hard fall" (Horton, 2011).

4.6 WHAT DOES IT MEAN IF YOUR SCHOOL HAS BEEN DESIGNATED AS "MILITARY FRIENDLY?"

You may have heard your students or administrators refer to your school as being "military friendly." However, if you really want to know what this phrase means, try reading a blog written by Capt. Robert Prah (2014), which appears on the U.S. Department of Veterans Affairs web site.

Prah, who serves in the Pennsylvania National Guard and is director of veterans affairs at California University of Pennsylvania, provides a brief explanation of this increasingly popular phrase, which he refers to as a marketing tool used by schools to attract military learners. Moreover, he offers some tips you might want to pass on to your students, including how to look beyond the logo and get concrete information about how many other veterans or military students are enrolled at the same institution (Prah, 2014).

4.7 USEFUL RESOURCES THAT CAN BE ACCESSED ONLINE

If you are an online instructor, one reader-friendly article that appeared in the education section of *U.S. News & World Report* provides ancedotal information from service members who are either in school or otherwise have advice to give other military learners who are still considering their options. Among the most beneficial features of this general news article are a former Marine veteran's tips on how to choose and succeed in a collegiate environment and encourage job prospects by getting involved in campus activities, and brief summaries about what to expect when taking courses in a community college setting. Some, if not most, of the information contained in this article can be shared with your students as well (Haynie, 2013).

Another online source that provides information you can use and share with your students is a web site hosted by the American Council on Education (ACE). ACE is an advocacy organization that includes representatives of colleges and universities across the country. ACE is contracted by the U.S. Department of Defense and administered by the Defense Activity for Non-Traditional Education Support (DANTES) to "conduct and facilitate academic reviews of military courses and occupations" (American Council on Education, 2016).

Under the tab titled "Higher Education Topics," are a range of briefs on getting military transcripts, deciding which courses to take and what types of careers to pursue, and understanding how veterans from different service units approach their undergraduate education. Because the site is comprehensive and provides so many detailed links to both empirical and anecdotal information, it is probably one that you want to keep on your "Favorites" list ("Military Students and Veterans," 2016).

4.8 RESOURCES YOUR STUDENTS CAN ACCESS ON THEIR OWN

Even though you want to play a supportive role in assisting your military students to identify a comprehensive list of services that are available to them, some of the sources are not geared directly for your use. Therefore, a sample of references that military learners can use to seek answers on their own follows.

When your students ask for advice about whether their military credits will transfer, you can refer them to the ACE web site, College Credit for Military Service (www.acenet.edu/higher-education/topics/Pages/College-Credit-for-Military-Service.aspx). Brief summaries and recommendations can be found on the following topics:

- A list of recommended courses and work-related skills that are most likely to qualify under college and university credit transfer policies.
- Explanations of how military transcripts are constructed and samples of related documents for each service division.
- A Q & A that responds to questions students may have about how a university will determine whether their skills and military training provide transferable credits. Subtopics include:
  - A discussion of whether correspondence courses, vocational training, and credits earned in military specialized occupations will be transferable.
  - A description of portfolio reviews that require students to document their military experiences to request credit for prior learning experiences.

The U.S. Department of Defense sponsors a web site that is a good starting point for both you and your students. However, more than likely, you are going to offer your students the URL so they can do research on their own. It is the Defense Activity for Non-Traditional Education Support (DANTES; www.military.com/education/timesaving-programs/defense-activity-for-non-traditional-education-support-dantes.html). And although you will be able to find up-to-date research on military education and links to federal government and individual service branch web sites, most of this information is geared directly toward your student and can actually be quite helpful.

Another very interesting and helpful site is TA DECIDE (www.dodmou.com/TADECIDE/). This DOD-sponsored site was set up in 2015, specifically to help service members decide which college to attend and whether they should enroll on a part-time or full-time basis. A comprehensives database of schools that have been "vetted" by the DOD includes institutions that can provide tuition assistance. By inputting basic information about location, type of learning platform desired, and choice of programs to pursue, this web site can provide a comparison of educational costs among several institutions.

Other resources that could definitely prove useful to your students include information on testing sites for entrance exams, career guidance, and explanations of how to become a teacher in a public school system. The DANTES Information Bulletin (DIB; www.dantes.doded.mil/dib.html) provides a monthly calendar on any program changes and new opportunities. This site is user friendly because the links are easy to identify and access. Many questions about either educational or professional interests can be easily answered within a very short span of time.

Another source titled "From Soldier to Student: Easing the Transition of Service Members on Campus" (www.acenet.edu/news-room/Documents/From-Soldier-to-Student-Easing-the-Transition-of-Service-Members-on-Campus.pdf) summarizes on-campus resources and institutional policies in place at colleges and universities nationwide that are geared toward assisting the military learner. The information will probably need to be supplemented with a more up-to-date source because this report was published in 2009.

Refer students who seem reluctant to ask you questions but are not actively participating in class to the web site Military OneSource (http://www.militaryonesource.mil). The funding for this site is provided by the U.S. Department of Defense, and the list of services offered to "active duty, Guard and Reserve Component members, and their families" is quite impressive.

Moreover, the site states that any counseling services are kept confidential, and range from emotional and physical to financial and marital issues. Grief counseling, job advice, concerns about deployment or reentering civilian life can also be discussed, and services can be accessed online or through a telephone hotline that operates twenty-four hours a day. No fees are charged ("About Military OneSource," 2016).

5

DEFINING THE NEEDS OF ONLINE MILITARY STUDENTS

5.1 USING TECHNOLOGY TO TRANSFORM HISTORY

Distance education represents a transformation in the delivery of core curriculum from a "traditional learning environment" to a more accessible and technologically oriented platform. In that regard, online military students are a unique subset of learners who directly benefit from the shift in pedagogy (Smucny & Stover, 2013).

One reason that military personnel can use this particular approach to learning so succesfully is that it offers them the flexibility they need to meet a demanding schedule, says Lt. Col. Thiem. "When you are deployed, there is work, and then there is eating and sleeping, and that is really the only things you do" (Thiem, 2016).

The only problem in such remote locations is that the ability to log into the online classroom is often restricted to the available amount of bandwidth. And sometimes, Thiem says, those limitations create difficulties with following the lesson plan because many times the majority of the bandwidth is used up by personnel who come back from the field and use the Internet to connect with their family and friends (Thiem, 2016).

Thiem, who has provided online instruction, said that teachers need to be understanding of the uncertainty that their military students face. For instance, if a person is deployed without much notice, he or she may not initially be able to make contact with the outside world during specific blocks of time and many times may not be able to log on to the Internet for at least a week after arrival at their new location.

Capt. Robert E. Rue Sr., who has been in the U.S. Army for nineteen years and has experienced an online learning environment from the perspective of both student and online instructor, states that a person who is deployed and accesses a computer from a remote location can also experience delayed participation in class discussions (Rue, 2015).

Then again, many deployed service members are likely to log into their classrooms via Internet cafes, which Rue refers to as "morale welfare and recreation" (MWR) facilities that operate on computer networks specifically designated for personal online activities. But, Rue adds, the connection can be difficult to maintain over extended periods of time because maximum usage in a combat zone is about thirty minutes (Rue, 2015).

Obviously, when such restrictions are imposed, the deployed service member can find it extremely difficult to participate in classroom discussions or to devote time to writing and revising written class assignments, as well as to complete online tests and quizzes. Limited access to the Internet can also interfere with the ability to deliver a quality research effort that is based on a thorough and comprehensive investigation of the topic at hand.

Moreover, in global regions where Internet access is subject to government regulations, a military learner's ability to use an online learning platform can be limited or restricted entirely. And deployed units can change locations so frequently that the ability to download online course materials can be difficult as well. Other challenges of logging in from a distant global region are that network speeds can be quite slow and time zone differences can lead to confusion about submitting assignments on time.

This chapter will offer you tips on locating resources for online students, such as mentors, tutors, or technical support staff members. Techniques that can be used by you or shared with your students about constructing advance notification of anticipated absences and requests for assistance with entering or navigating the online classroom will be provided as well.

5.2 TECHNOLOGY AND TEACHING: KEEPING AN OPEN MIND

The U.S. Department of Defense Voluntary Education Partnership Memorandum of Understanding (MOU) specifies that a learning institution must provide military students with policy information on adding, dropping, or withdrawing from a course; necessary steps to gain readmittance; and how unexpected military duties such as deployment can impact academic standing and loan obligations (Sweizer, n.d.).

How do these requirements impact the online learning environment? Unlike in a traditional brick-and-mortar classroom, one of the key facts to keep in mind when teaching online is that the platform is conducive to establishing flexibility of course guidelines and assignment submission requirements in the syllabus, opening announcements, and e-mails to students.

Also, because self-discipline and self-motivation are required skills to participate in an online classroom, the lack of a formal meeting place and regular interactions with other students can lead to challenges for service members who are trying to complete their required coursework on time (Rue, 2015).

Veterans can experience certain obstacles, as well, as a result of conditions such as post-traumatic stress disorder (PTSD) and traumatic brain injuries, depressive disorders, and reoccurring negative or suicidal thoughts (VA Campus Toolbook, 2012). According to Alex Horton, who is a public affairs specialist at the Department of Veterans Affairs and an English major at Georgetown University, more than 50 percent of service members report having witnessed scenes of dead bodies or "human remains," or having known someone who has either died or suffered serious injuries during conflict situations (Horton, 2011).

They may also experience a corresponding sense of loss (Horton, 2011), which can interfere with their ability to concentrate, or to focus on the achievement of their academic goals (VA Campus Toolbook, 2012). Additional feelings of guilt or blame can similarly interfere with their comprehension levels and reading skills (Chickering & Gamson, 1987). All of these issues can impact the veteran's capacity to sustain focus on course material or to study for exams.

However, the most common physical constraints that can impact the veteran learner's ability to sit for prolonged periods of time or to use a keyboard are musculoskeletal problems as a result of amputations, back pain, difficulty in range of motion, or hearing problems. Moreover, the side effects of certain medications or treatments can interfere with making the time commitment necessary to complete online discussions and to submit assignments according to specified deadlines. In addition, problems with hearing can have significant impacts if the instructor chooses to conduct webinars or requires students to communicate via an online platform that requires the use of both auditory and visual comprehension skills (VA Campus Toolbook, 2012).

Horton (2011) points out that some undergraduate school administrators discourage veteran students from enrolling if they are not able to focus solely on their academic pursuits. However, he also indicates that veterans have learned during their years of military service to rise above such challenges. "We (veterans) are hard-wired to complete missions quickly and efficiently, but we need universities to understand and anticipate our unique circumstances. We are here to fulfill a new mission. It just happens to be a degree" (Horton, 2011).

Like veteran learners, spouses of service members have their own issues with using an online learning platform. "When you are married to an active-duty service member, you can move an average of every two to three years," said Karen Golden, deputy director of government relations for MOAA. She adds that the average spouse is female, thirty-three years old, has either some college education or has completed her bachelor's degree, and is likely to have children, be unemployed, or make 33 percent less than her civilian counterpart (Golden, 2015).

Another category of military learners who experience challenges in an online learning environment are Reservists and National Guardsmen. These individuals are required to participate in drill training one weekend a month and an additional two weeks during the year. Meanwhile, they cope with the stress of not knowing when and where they could suddenly be deployed (VA Campus Toolbook, 2013).

In reality, both Reservists and National Guardsmen are being called to active duty more and more frequently. "When I went through my undergraduate degree in 1983–1987, I was in the Army National Guard," Thiem says. "There was not even a thought that you would be going to war; that you would be deployed; that was not even a thought process." But, "[t]hat is just not the same anymore," and reservists are likely to be called to active duty now as well (Thiem, 2016).

Their participation in the online environment can be affected if their location or their access to computers suddenly changes (VA Campus Toolbook, 2012). And, if deployed, they can lose their private-sector salaries, which consequently can greatly reduce their individual or family income. Moreover, the sudden adjustment to being away from their family members can demand a tremendous emotional adjustment as well (Ermold, 2013).

5.3 FROM A DESIGNER'S POINT OF VIEW

If you have worked in an online platform before, you know that two options are generally available to you:

- design your own curriculum, or
- use the course material that has been already developed by your learning institution.

If the former option exists, you also know that creating online course material, which is both user friendly and well received by your students, is not necessarily an easy task. And, Thiem suggests, when a class roster is likely to include the names of military personnel, you are advised to identify these individuals right away. "I think that positively affects the student's ability to complete his course of study if he or she feels that the instructor has an understanding of the issues that might impact his or her ability to complete the course." But he says that students are also responsible in ensuring that their learning needs are met as well. Therefore, they need to contact you as early in the term as possible to let you know if they could be recalled to duty or deployed for the first time. Thiem also advises you to create a structured schedule that details each course component and make this information available to military students when the class begins (Thiem, 2016).

Moreover, according to Fanella (2016), your success is often determined by your adaptability to new technologies. If you are more resistant to the structure of an online learning platform, you are likely to experience greater frustrations. On the other hand, the more knowledge you have about how to use specific software that delivers online course information, the better able you are able to make the transition from a brick-

and-mortar classroom to a virtual teaching environment. "You sort of have to anticipate questions that might be asked," Fanella (2016) says. "That is just a skill which has to be learned."

But, he adds, the predictions that current generations would be techno-savvy by the time online platforms were in full utilization were only partially realized because many students still prefer to print out their course materials and have their textbooks in hand. "You are getting students who are sort of 50/50; some want everything online, while the other part of the population want to print everything out and read it," Fanella (2016) says.

He describes the type of curriculum he designs as "military strategic content," which means it is intended for high-ranking officers who are working on their graduate degrees. Among the challenge he faces is making sure the course content can be disseminated in the various media the student population is demanding. Fanella also takes pride in refuting a perception that the majority of military students lack any formal education past high school. "If you take a look at all the officers in all four branches of the military; all of them have to have a degree. And there are processes in place for them to get their master's degree," Fanella (2016) says, adding that the War College is not the only senior-level educational institution able to grant master's degrees.

Enlisted service members usually sign up after high school, where they receive extensive training. The period of their enlistment varies depending on factors such as what the military's needs are, their training agreements, and whether they receive either an enlistment or a reenlistment bonus. But often the enlistment period is about four years or longer, and the average age of someone who leaves the military after their first enlistment is often in their mid-twenties. However, the choice to reenlist usually also means that the service member is likely to continue to be promoted and is likely to have achieved the rank of a sergeant.

Fanella (2016) says his job is also to make sure the instructor's technical proficiency is consistent with the course demands. "Faculty development not only consists of how to teach from the instructional standpoint, but also how to use the technology to get your job done," he says.

When he began working for the Army War College, Fanella says that course instructors would hand him the content and he would then package that information for online delivery. Typically, the materials were disseminated in the form of web pages. But, he adds that some instructors at that time just did not have the technical proficiency needed for an online platform. "About ten years ago, we had this course author who came down to my office with her hair on fire. She was just livid, and demanded to know how I could have put her course online, when none of the videos had sound."

Fanella said he checked the sound system on three or four computers, to first confirm that it was working. Then he went to speak to the instructor again and noticed her headphones were plugged into the speaker, but that she had forgotten to place the equipment on her head.

"So I walked over and unplugged the headphones from the speaker, and said to her, 'Try the videos right now.' Of course, they worked."

Today, Fanella still faces the challenge of being able to identify what type of information to include in course content and how much of that learning material can actually be disseminated to the student population because topics can range from a general discussion of current events to a disclosure of top-secret information. And once he has finished developing the curriculum, he still uses the same procedure of disseminating that information for instructional use.

5.4 KNOWING "RIGHT" FROM "WRONG"

In a 2012 press release released by the White House, President Barack Obama announced official policy changes that were designed to respond to "reports of aggressive and deceptive targeting of service members, veterans, and their families by some educational institutions." In this same announcement, he identified how his Executive Order would help service members, veterans, spouses, and other family members get a quality education when using their post–9/11 GI Bill benefits.

Obama's concerns included the following: "Some institutions have recruited veterans with serious brain injuries and emotional vulnerabilities without providing academic support and practices on military installations; and failed to disclose meaningful information that allows potential students to determine whether the institution has a good record of graduating service members, veterans, and their families and positioning them for success in the workforce" (Obama, 2012).

Among the criteria for change President Obama emphasized in his legislative mandate are the principles of "oversight," "enforcement," and accountability" for all schools that are providing education to military students and receiving tuition monies paid through benefit programs. He also authorized the creation of a web page on the U.S. Department of Veterans Affairs site that offers a comparison of:

- school costs and benefits, including statistics on tuition and housing allowances;
- identification of whether academic credit is given for military training;
- "the median of former students who received federal financial aid, at 10 years after entering school"; and,
- samples of student complaints about specific academic institutions (Obama, 2012).

Such efforts appear to be paying off, as more and more schools are forced into a position of accountability for their treatment of military learners.

Thiem (2016) offers his own advice about how online learners should consider the selection of a school. The first rule is to determine if the school is accredited. The second is to review the components of the online learning program and see how the courses compare to the same program that is offered in a classroom setting.

"I would also look for a program that has the capability of transferring from an in-residence program to an online option," he says. "If you get deployed, I would look at the overall cost as well, since I know that the military caps the amount that it will pay per credit. There is no reason to go outside of a well-respected program that fits within the cost."

Moreover, Thiem also admits that although online course delivery has gotten progressively better over the years, the "human element" is not as strong as it is in a brick-and-mortar setting.

"There is something about interacting with other humans that enhances the learning process," he says. You miss out on that in an online program because often you learn as much from your fellow students as you do from your instructors" (Thiem, 2016).

6

WHO IS THE ARMY LEARNER?

I hate war as only a soldier who has lived it can, only as one who has seen its brutality, its stupidity.
–President Dwight D. Eisenhower

6.1 WHO JOINS THIS BRANCH OF THE SERVICE AND WHY?

Be honest. Most of you reading this chapter may have never really considered joining the military or analyzed the sacrifices inherent in conscripting four years of your life to living in remote desert regions, or learned how to load and shoot a weapon in front of an armed opponent.

Why would you? You have a career; you have an education; and, more than likely, you have a bit of comfort in your physical surroundings as well. More than that, however, you have selected a path that places you in a leadership position, where your knowledge is respected and your skills are reflected in your title, salary, or level of seniority within your academic institution.

So if one of your military students approaches you or sends you an e-mail saying that he or she has orders to deploy, your immediate response is likely to be among the following:

- Sympathetic
- Empathetic
- Concerned from an abstract point of view

- Can't be bothered because all of your students face challenges that are associated with their academic pursuits.

6.1.1 History Offers Different Conclusions

Regardless of your response, you could reasonably regard this matter as being of little consequence because your experiences and those of your military students may have created an artificial divide.

According to military advocate and former Marine Sergeant Alexander Baldwin McCoy "American society has a very clear cultural stereotype of a service member as a southern conservative white male, who is typically masculine, and the reality is that many female military personnel and veterans often struggle with being dismissed. Thus, like any student identity, it is important to empower that individual to express his or her ideas, rather than to assume what someone's viewpoint will be" (McCoy, 2016).

Looking back at history, however, the scenario just described could have produced a different outcome, because, not that long ago, the realities of those who entered the military and those who did not were not as obvious. What has forced this division to occur is apparently "a mutual distrust between the American military and civilian worlds," according to Donald A. Zinman in his review of *AWOL: The Unexcused Absence of America's Upper Classes from Military Service—and How It Hurts Our Country*, by K. Roth-Douquet and F. Schaeffer (2010).

Yet your perceptions of what your military students are like are probably not that different from the stereotypical ideas they may have about you before they enter your classroom. You are probably a "too-far-to-the-left" liberal, who views military students as war mongers and believes that they carry guns as a sign of their machismo. Moreover, you may perceive their perpetual silence during classroom discussions as a sign that they probably disagree with everything you say, and because you have lived a sheltered and somewhat limited existence, you can't possibly understand the sacrifices many military students go through to even afford a seat in your classroom. You might also have preconceived ideas about how bright these students are and how capable they are of keeping up with their nonmilitary classmates.

6.1.2 Overcoming the Impasse

To build a bridge to understanding that will help eliminate any preconceived ideas that your military students may have about you, or vice versa, the first step is to learn who these students are and what their professional responsibilities require them to do.

Perhaps you are old enough to remember a song performed by Abe Lyman and his Californians, with vocals by The Chorus that was recorded during World War II, and later transformed into a children's rhyme. The first verse is probably the one most familiar to you: "We're in the Army now / We're not behind a plow / We'll never get rich diggin' a ditch / We're in the Army now" ("WWII in American Music: Pre-War Defense," 2012). These lyrics are meant to reflect the military past. But do these images represent the military *today* as well?

Even without enlisting, you can still determine those answers by looking at the kind of information that potential Army enlistees are urged to ask their recruiters before agreeing to sign their names above the dotted line.

Before you glance through the next subsection, try to challenge yourself a bit by seeing if you can answer the questions posed in each of the division titles.

6.1.3 How Is This Branch of the Service Different from Any Other?

If you read through the criteria for joining the Army, you might want to ask yourself, "Would I be able to qualify?" For instance, for those of you who are online instructors and spend more time in the front of the computer than on an exercise machine, perhaps the initial requirement of having to pass a physical exam would be difficult to meet. But even if you are a bit challenged by a few extra pounds, you can sometimes get in, with the proviso that you are definitely going to have to reduce that muffin top during your tour of duty.

Both men and women can join the Army, though women cannot serve in combat roles. While your application is being considered, you cannot smoke pot or take other drugs, seriously imbibe alcohol, or demonstrate any type of criminal behavior. Forget those tongue piercings too, because they will definitely disqualify you. Consider, too, that if you decided to get a tattoo during your "wild and crazy" days of youth, you will not be considered "fit" to join the Army if these decorations are located on your head, face, neck, wrists, hands, or fingers.

Moreover, the concept of whether you exhibit "questionable moral behavior" will definitely be an issue as well. You have to be able to document every traffic ticket or other minor offense that you have committed over your lifetime. On the positive side, you can still get in if you can use the technique of persuasive argument to convince your recruiter that your days of ignoring parking meters or rolling through stop signs are things of the past.

The age requirements to join could an inhibiting factor as well because you have to be eighteen to join, but cannot be older than thirty-five. And for those of you who have preconceived ideas about your military students' educational experiences to join the Army, you are pretty much disqualified unless you have a high school diploma, or GED, and at least fifteen college credits. In addition, commissioned officers are not allowed to assume their responsibilities unless they have obtained at least a bachelor's degree.

Finally, the recruiter may not even begin to process your application if you are married and have at least two other people who depend on you for support (plus "one on the way," if your wife is pregnant).

6.1.4 What Makes a Soldier a Soldier?

Ten weeks. That is how long a new recruit is required to commit to complete basic training. Gone are the days of mall shopping and worrying about color-matching clothes. Instead, you will only be allowed to bring one complete outfit, three sets of white underwear, a pair of white athletic socks (no Nike emblems allowed), one pair of comfortable shoes, a utilitarian pair of eyeglasses, and a small suitcase or gym bag. End of story. Hair dryers are not permitted, and either a brush or comb is allowed, but not both.

Moreover, do not worry about draining your bank account if you decide to join the Army because new recruits can only bring a total of fifty dollars cash when they present their orders and reports for training. Once they receive their uniform, they begin to undergo repeated tests of physical endurance. They also learn about the challenges of confronting chemical and nuclear weapons, how to tread lightly around land mines, and the art of tying a rope around their waist and learning to gracefully descend from "nose-bleeding heights," strictly for survival purposes.

And so, on to the next level of physical endurance training where the soldier becomes a marathon marcher and expert marksman. They also face the challenge of completing obstacle courses, which are unlike any you may have encountered in a school gym class.

As the recruit trains, they literally begin to take on a new persona by completing actions that are diametrically opposed to traits they displayed in civilian life. No longer can they tune out daily stress with computer headphones or chats online. Now they must face the harsh realities of war by loading and firing machine guns and throwing a hand grenade. And if all goes well during this ten-week period of initial training, they graduate and prepare themselves for more specialized and individualized instruction.

The skills learned in these next set of courses are consistent with both college and vocational training and may also include vehicle maintenance, human resources, fire protection, emergency medical care, communications, and intelligence. Of course, each of these training programs is geared toward improving the soldier's ability to perform their responsibilities in the Army.

Once trained, the enlisted soldier is now ready to report to duty. If they decide to make active duty a full-time commitment, they will generally be in the service for two to six years. But if they choose to enter the Reserves, they can still maintain their civilian jobs, while fulfilling their military commitments on a part-time basis for twelve months to six years. If the need warrants, however, reservists can be called to active duty.

6.1.5 Duty Calls: Missing Assignments Due to Deployment

You may have already encountered a situation in which a student unexpectedly e-mails you right before an assignment is due, indicating that he or she is about to be deployed. How do you respond or know if this student is just using his or her military commitments to get extra time to complete work?

First of all, the student is letting you know that a decision has been made *for* him or her, instead of made *by* him or her, and therefore, there is a 99.99 percent chance that this e-mail reflects a matter of real urgency, rather than an excuse for a missing assignment.

But do you really know what the term *deployment* means, or how these circumstances affect the particular student who has sent you this e-mail? Deployment means that the student has received orders that he or she—and his or her unit—is probably going to leave American soil and travel to another country or conflict region where he or she may be asked to participate in one or more of the following activities:

- Combat
- Disaster relief
- Humanitarian efforts

The deployment can last up to two years, and when the student writes the e-mail to you, he or she may or may not know to what destination he or she has been assigned, nor how soon after departure that he or she will be able to access the Internet again.

Soldiers in the Army National Guard and Army Reserve can also be deployed. However, when the need for their services lessens, their commitment returns to a part-time status and they generally return home.

6.2 GOALS IN PURSUING AN EDUCATION

By 2020, more than five million post–9/11 service members are likely to be attempting to reintegrate into the private sector, according to the U.S. Government Accountability Office (Molina & Morse, 2015). And if they choose to enroll in your classroom, they will probably observe that about 95 percent of their classmates have no prior military experience, according to statistics provided by the U.S. Department of Education's National Center for Education Statistics (Molina & Morse, 2015).

If one of your students indicates that he or she has recently joined the Army, is currently a member of that service branch, or has completed his or her tour of duty, you may wonder why he or she has now chosen to pursue a college degree. If the student is still on active duty, the answer is that his or her ability to successfully complete college courses has a direct impact on his or her capacity to be promoted in the ranks. In fact, the Army's method of promotion, which is based on a point system, allocates the most points possible for degree completion (GoArmy.com).

WHO IS THE ARMY LEARNER?

Some veterans also specifically entered the service so that they could get enough money to get a college education and now they are able to realize that goal. Others want to learn how to reorient themselves to a civilian lifestyle that is more in tune with who they have become through the depth of their military experiences and expertise (Lighthall, n.d.).

6.3 A QUESTION OF SEMANTICS

For those of you who teach professional writing courses, one of the most challenging aspects of your job is introducing your students to formatting styles that are consistent with business correspondences. On a smaller scale, you may have to explain the differences in capitalizing a person's title before or after a name, or the reason why grammar rules do not apply to an organizational name or logo.

Now consider that the same learning curve is being applied to you within the pages of this text. Thus, if the question "How many types of soldiers are there in the Army?" were posed to you, do you think you could provide the correct answer? Maybe not. However, in fact there are three:

- enlisted soldiers,
- warrant officers, and
- commissioned officers.

Going back to the issue of preparing a lecture on professional communication, one of the basic questions you would probably ask your students is do they know what a CEO does and what leadership skills he or she must possess to obtain that type of a high-ranking position?

But what if the tables were turned, and instead, the following question was posed to you: "Do you know what skills distinguish one solider from another, and which has the higher rank?" Again, if you are finding that you are unable to achieve a passing grade on this an informal quiz, you are probably receiving the same scores as many other instructors.

Consider that 3 percent of the Army's personnel are warrant officers, and these individuals must be able to multitask. Thus, during their advanced training, they have pursued such technical fields as intelligence, aviation, or becoming a member of the military police. They also are required to train other soldiers and serve as mission advisers while they continue to strengthen their professional skills.

Commissioned officers also play a leadership role in the training process of enlisted soldiers, as well as in the planning of missions. The talent needed for such a position has been recognized in such iconic historical figures as George Washington, Ulysses S. Grant, George Patton, Dwight D. Eisenhower, and, more recently, former U.S. Secretary of State and member of the Joint Chiefs of Staff, Colin Powell.

Additionally, regardless of where a solider is stationed, most Army posts include satellite campuses of local universities. Because these schools are directly connected to the central campus, earned credits count toward a degree from that institution.

Veterans usually decide to pursue their degrees in order to improve their chances of finding a decent-paying job in the private sector and to transition into mainstream society more smoothly. But many veterans have a hard time completing their college education, which could contribute to the fact that an estimated 130,000 to 200,000 homeless in the United States were formerly members of the U.S. Armed Services, according to the National Coalition for the Homeless (Kness & O'Neill, 2016).

Women who have served account for 2 million members of this population, and the U.S. Department of Veterans Affairs states they are among the most likely groups to end up living on the streets (Kness & O'Neill, 2016).

One factor that could reduce the drop-out rate for veterans is a more recent trend in providing college credits for past experiences. Thus, some schools offer these students the chance to submit a written portfolio that illustrates their level of knowledge and ability that corresponds to specific course outcomes. According to the County for Adult and Experiential Learning (CAEL), students who are able to quality for such credits are 2.5 times as likely to graduate than veterans who do not have these credentials. Such efforts to provide credit for military training and experiences are now backed by legislation in twenty-six states.

Several studies indicate that veterans who do enroll in school have a greater chance of obtaining their goals than their civilian counterparts. Additionally, one factor that is said to increase their success rate is the presence of "faculty who are sensitive to military culture" (National Conference of State Legislatures, 2014).

6.4 FACTORS AFFECTING GRADUATION SUCCESS

According to a report released by the Student Affairs Administrators in Higher Education (NASPA) Policy Institute and Inside Track, no accurate numbers are available that can predict how many of your students are likely to be either active-duty service members or veterans. The same issue exists in terms of identifying how many of these students are likely to drop out of your class or leave the school altogether before completing their degrees. Although the survey results do indicate that many institutions are making a more concerted effort to help these military students (NASPA Research and Policy Institute in partnership with Inside Track, 2013), your approach to these learners can and will definitely affect their potential to succeed in a postsecondary educational environment.

6.5 SUCCESS RATE IN THE PRIVATE SECTOR AND TYPES OF CAREERS OFTEN PURSUED

Transitioning back to the private sector does not end with the obtainment of a college degree. Being able to find a job translates to establishing independence and being able to financially support a family. The organizations teach for America and Troops for Teachers both have a nationwide presence, and their goal is to help veterans obtain their teaching credentials and be placed in the classroom (National Conference of State Legislatures, 2014).

7

WHO IS THE MARINE LEARNER?

7.1 WHO JOINS THIS BRANCH OF THE SERVICE AND WHY?

If you see a service member in uniform, can you actually identify which military branch he or she belongs to? Perhaps not. But, for future reference, a male or female who is sporting a flat white cap with a shiny black rim, a crew cut (men) or short hair that is well-trimmed or generally pulled back in a tight ponytail (women), a tan or light brown short-sleeved shirt with crisp creases in each of the arms, and a pair of straight-legged black pants with a bright red stripe running down both legs, is probably a Marine.

You may have heard the common expression that the Marines are the toughest fighting branch in the U.S. Armed Forces. Before you decide if this statement is true, read the description of this organization's mission provided on the Marines' official web site, under the Recruit Training.

> "No Free Ride"
> It is appropriate that a river as defining as the mighty Mississippi determines the path for those who aspire to defend our great country. Reside east of her (Mississippi) and your bus arrives at Marine Corps Recruit Depot Parris Island in South Carolina, where sand fleas await in open swamps. Reside west, and your bus doesn't stop until it reaches Marine Corps Recruit Depot San Diego and the unforgiving hills of Southern California, where aching muscles and burning lungs become as familiar as the landscape. All female recruits arrive at Parris Island.

Regardless of which Depot you reach, the path ahead is equally intense. Those who prevail after 12 demanding weeks will emerge completely transformed, prepared to defend our country and each other.

So, what do you think? Is joining the Marines more challenging than riding the New York subway to your 8 AM class or adjusting to a new software that your employer has decided to implement two weeks before your next term starts?

The United States Marine Corps (USMC) was authorized to defend the United States "on sea and on shore" in 1775 and is still considered to be "our nation's first line of defense" (www.marines.com). The Marine Corps operate as a separate service branch under the U.S. Department of the Navy and completes frequent missions that require cooperation of both service branches (Szoldra, 2013).

But the doctors, nurses and other medical personnel who treat Marines who have been wounded in combat are actually Navy personnel. Also although this service unit may employ the fewest members of any armed services branch, they also have the longest basic training requirements, and deployment is guaranteed ("10 Things to Consider When Joining The Marines," 2016).

Consider, too, that the Marines operate a ground task force that includes officers who are trained pilots. So, Marines serve both on Navy ships and fly helicopters and planes. Their numbers are much smaller than the Army's because their focus is on responding to international conflicts as quickly as possible. The Army, on the other hand, particpates in longer and larger conflicts and has the capacity to take over the security and safety efforts that the Marines have intiated by being the United State's first line of defense. "Marines serve on U.S. Navy ships, protect naval bases, guard U.S. embassies, and provide an ever-ready quick strike force to protect U.S. interests anywhere in the world" ("Answers to the Top Marine Corps Questions," n.d.).

7.1.1 Conditions of Enlistment and Goals in Pursuing an Education

But even if you are feeling a patriotic urge to serve your country right now, it is probably best not to quit your day job just yet. Consider that even if you are younger than thirty and can therefore easily meet the age requirements, you still have to score well on the test of physical strength. And this is not the kind of exam that you are probably used to, in terms of lifting your favorite brand of diet soda to your lips as you swipe your fingers gracefully back and forth across the computer keyboard to prepare your next lesson plan. This test requires you to demonstrate your dexterity, temerity, and your ability to exceed your physical limits, at least temporarily.

So, before you commit yourself to completing forty-four grueling stomach crunches in 120 seconds, better check that expanding waistline. Also, your ability to run from the most distant region of the parking lot to your next class will not really qualify you to for the requisite 1.5-mile run that is required here as well. Oh, and you may want to check with your doctor to make sure that your physique meets the required body mass index standards as well. Ouch. And that is just the list of entry-level requirements.

If you want to choose the training program that will prepare you to become an officer, the official Marines' web site recommends adding lunges, dips (and not onion or guacamole!), sit-ups, shoulder presses, back extensions, leg lifts, heel raises, and bicep curls to your three-day-a-week preparatory routine for at least one year. (No advice is given on seeking medical attention if your strength gives out "mid-push-up.") All this training is required to earn the privilege of pronouncing the Latin phrase: *SEMPER FIDELIS*.

Now, enough discussion of exercise. If a Marine came into your classroom in full uniform, would you know how to address him or her by rank and title, and would you consider such matters relevant to your professional responsibilities? Perhaps it is better to respond to each of these questions separately.

If your first guess about your student's title is that he or she is an enlisted recruit, you are probably right because the majority of Marines fit into that category, and their ranks range from private to sergeant major. On the other hand, if your student has trained as an officer, his or her rank will range from second lieutenant to four-star general. Thus, if you are unsure how to address your student, you are better off just asking whether he or she is an enlisted service member or a commissioned officer and what specific rank. By asking questions about your students, you are letting them know that you are interested in their welfare and participation in your classroom.

Marines have separate educational requirements for enlisted service members and officers. The former must have either a high school diploma or GED or be in the process of completing these requirements. Officers must have a bachelor's degree to earn commission and rank. Somewhat like the Army, Marines must attend boot camp and then complete occupational training in more specialized fields such as infantry, aircraft maintenance, and explosive ordnance disposal. Enlisted recruits also have the potential to rise to an officer's rank if they can meet the qualifications ("Glossary of Career Education Programs," n.d.). And, similar to the Army, the Marine Corps has Reserve units as well.

8

WHO IS THE NAVY LEARNER?

To be prepared for war is one of the most effective means of preserving peace.
–General George Washington

8.1 WHO JOINS THIS BRANCH OF THE SERVICE AND WHY?

Most Americans perceive the Navy as the least essential of the armed services, according to the results of a 2014 Gallup poll results reported in the *International Business Times*. But which military branch launched a clandestine operation that resulted in the execution of former al-Qaeda leader Osama Bin Laden? Why, the Navy, of course (Massi, 2014).

If you decide to join the Navy or Navy Reserves, the type of knot-tying skills you will learn are better suited if you have summers off to enjoy boating and camping activities in the great outdoors. And if you teach in coastal regions where shark sightings trigger panic attacks on a fairly frequent basis, the Navy teaches you how to float when someone on the boat yells, "Man [person?] overboard." You can also learn to use your clothes as flotation devices. (Would Armani suits or Anne Taylor be acceptable?) If you feel that your swim stroke is a bit rusty, the Navy will show you how to get those biceps in shape so that you can safely make a break toward dry land.

There is even a course for women (or men) who believe that finding your way around the kitchen is essentially a medieval task. According to the Navy's official web site, you will learn "a few simple but worthwhile cooking skills and quick recipes from professionally trained Culinary Specialists." Would this training regimen qualify you to work as a cook at a fancy restaurant? Probably not, but what the heck, you never know until you try. (What happened to Spam in a can served three times a day?)

If you grew up in a region of the country where the misquotes resemble torpedo bombers, the Navy's Hospital Corpsmen offer you survival training techniques so that you do not "succumb to the elements." Finally, when you take that once-a-year hike through the mountains and realize that tall trees or ornamental grasses do not make reliable trail markers, the Navy teaches you how to build shelters, send out a distress signal when needed, and survive in the wilderness until help arrives ("Navy Skills for Life," n.d.). (If you are forty or older and admit to watching *Gilligan's Island*, this training may remind you of those televised images from yesteryears.)

So, when and if you do decide to join the Navy, you are going to be learning defense techniques that apply to both land and sea. Moreover, you can opt to enlist as a sailor, or, if you have already obtained your degree, you can decide to attend officer training school. What may also prove interesting is that the Navy's web site appears to be heavily oriented toward appealing to a civilian audience, unlike the sites for some other service branches. Thus, the language is much more consistent with the type of marketing campaign that will entice a reluctant recruit to abandon remote controls or iPod ear plugs for a military uniform and the chance to defend the country against foreign and domestic enemies. And, if you still have a bit of wunderlust in your own soul, you may want to rent *The Hunt For Red October*, or *Crimson Tide* to see if you could survive in the close confined quarters of a submarine.

8.1.1 A Woman's Role Is in The Navy

> I am not afraid of storms, for I am learning how to sail my ship.
> –Louisa May Alcott

While women still earn 7 cents on the dollar that every man earns in this country, one place where sexism is being fought on open battlegrounds appears to be in the Navy. Signs of this progress include President Obama's historic appointment of Michelle Howard, the first black person and woman to serve in the capacity of a four-star Navy general. Not only that, but the last four decades have welcomed an 800 percent increase in the number of women serving in the military, which equates to about 18 percent of the workforce (Braun, 2015; "Navy Celebrates 2016 Women's History Month," 2015).

Women were permitted to serve in submarines as of 2010 (Comerford, 2011), and in January of 2016, they became eligible for combat duty and Special Forces units, like the Navy Seals ("Navy Celebrates 2016 Women's History Month," 2015). However, it also seems that the move toward equality is not necessarily enticing an abundance of female applicants for certain types of Seal training. Perhaps that is partly because to serve in the Basic Underwater Demolition Unit the applicant must be able to do the following:

- swim 1000 meters, with fins, in twenty-two minutes or less;
- complete seventy push-ups in two minutes;
- finish ten pull-ups in two minutes;
- perform sixty curl-ups in two minutes; and
- run four miles, wearing shoes and pants, in less than thirty minutes.

Perhaps the rigor of training required by the Navy and other service branches is why *Business Insider* reported that over 65 percent of young Americans would just not qualify. The major reasons cited for disqualification are "physical, behavioral, or educational problems," and, the most common concern about finding qualified recruits is the rising epidemic of obeisty that exists in this country (Stilwell, 2015).

8.1.2 The Navy from an "Academic Perspective"

Statistics on how many college and university instructors have joined the All-Volunteer Force (AVF) are not readily available. Yet the tale of one economics professor illustrates just how far apart the two worlds—academia and the service—really are. In 2010, Dr. Eric Schuck made the courageous decision to temporarily suspend his lecturing responsibilities in favor of joining the Navy Reserves. His experiences were chronicled by Pulitzer Prize–winning journalist Thomas Ricks in 2012. During the interview, which appeared in the "Voice" section of *Foreignpolicy.com*,

Schuck reveals the following impressions on his return from the service to academia:

> When other professors talk about my deployment, they describe it either as if I had the worst sabbatical ever, or as if I had taught in some horribly misguided semester at sea. They simply cannot bring themselves to say—or to acknowledge—that one of their own went to war. Such things are simply not dreamt of in their philosophies.

Professor Schuck joined the Navy Reserves and became Lt. Schuck, SC, USNR. He chose to trade in his cup of green tea for a sailor's uniform due to a deep sense of patriotism, a strong desire to serve his country, and a great respect for the Navy's mission.

He also appears to chastise his colleagues, who he believes are highly unlikely to trade their digital pointers and PowerPoint presentations for a sailor's uniform, when he comments that "Civilian society encourages the creation of a 'warrior caste' because it frees them of the guilt of not serving." And, in remarking on his subsequent return to teaching economics at Linfield College in Oregon, Schuck states that he now feels comparable to the literary concept of "the other" (Ricks, 2012).

8.1.3 Conditions of Enlistment and Goals in Pursuing an Education

A Navy recruit can learn to sail, pilot and fix an airplane, crew a submarine, scuba dive into very deep waters, and swim extremely fast and for long periods of time as well as to sky dive. In addition, he or she can learn how to use weapons and explosives during conflict situations. The Navy also provides transport services for the Marines (Smith, 2016).

The typical length of deployment for a sailor is about three years. During that time, sailors can be required to remain aboard a ship or submarine for six to nine months, before returning to shore for an interim six months for additional training (Smith, 2016).

Many sailors opt to leave the Navy or decide not to reenlist because they experience the same type of burn out that anyone does who has an extremely demanding job. Also they want to devote time to completing their degree or to raising their families. But obviously the Navy does not want fewer well-trained personnel, so a new innovative program was developed to allow officers, as well as enlisted members, to get the best of both worlds.

The Career Intermission Program lets sailors receive much-reduced pay in exchange for the opportunity to take an interim leave of up to three years. Enlisted members who want to take this option cite the desire to obtain a degree as one of their top priorities (Myers, 2015).

9

WHO IS THE AIR FORCE LEARNER?

9.1 WHO JOINS THIS BRANCH OF THE SERVICE AND WHY?

If you want to quickly distinguish the Air Force from other branches of the service, here are some basic differences, according to Bill Stein, former Air Force communication officer:

1. The food is better.
2. The fighting component is generally more technologically based, rather than focused on applied techniques of direct physical contact.
3. This service branch is the youngest, making its debut in 1947.
4. An ability to respond to the mission supersedes physical fitness requirements.

In fact, the mission of the Air Force sounds a bit ethereal when compared to the goals laid out by the other services branches. "To fly, fight and win in air, space and cyberspace" could just as well be a description of the National Aeronautics and Space Administration's objectives (www.airforce.com).

Moreover, explanations of how the Air Force fulfills its mission are reminiscent of a George Lucas film. For instance, one of the primary objectives is to achieve "rapid global mobility," in case of the need for a global strike. (Perhaps the Air Force should consider renaming itself "The Force," in honor of the iconic film which demonstrated to the world how such tasks can be performed.) And the Air Force appears to be producing effective results because no enemy combat aircraft has taken the life of a single U.S service member operating in the ground forces since April 15, 1953 ("Air Force Core Missions," n.d.).

Greatly adding to the space-age image of the Air Force is the web site's description of how it "deploys and operates six constellations and over 170 satellites." The objectives of these extraterrestrial fighting forces are to monitor activity on the ground and in the atmosphere. So the Air Force operates these remote-control cameras continuously from the air, taking pictures or conducting video surveillance.

Consider that this service branch is capable of deploying "flexible, precise, and lethal force" to any region of the globe ("Message From CASF," n.d.). But one fact about the Air Force that appears to be somewhat oxymoronic is that only 13 percent of its members actually fly airplanes ("What are good reasons for joining the Air Force rather than the Army or the Navy?" 2015).

In addition, the cultural norm appears to support references to both male and female pilots as "airmen" on the Air Force's official web site. Airmen are ranked differently than officers; although, the higher the number, the more responsibility and pay the service member receives.

Another interesting fact about the Air Force is that its educational system appears to operate more like a traditional university structure than similar systems offered by other service branches. After eight and a half weeks of basic training, the new recruit must then report to technical school, and receive career training. Each course that is completed with a passing grade counts as credit toward a degree from the Community College of the Air Force (CCAF).

Describing itself as the "world's largest community college system," the CCAF has established partnerships with more than 1,500 educational institutions that have no direct military affiliations and offer sixty-eight degree programs. Moreover, more than 22,000 students a year receive their associate's degree in applied science ("Welcome to the Community College of the Air Force," 2015).

9.1.1 A Force to Be Reckoned with

Like all branches of the military, the Air Force is continuing to evolve with the times. For instance, the first woman entered a pilot training program in 1976, navigator training in 1977, and fighter pilot training in 1993. Now, 19 percent of the force is comprised of women; about 20 percent of women are enlisted, and 20 percent have achieved officer rank. Moreover, the Air Force counts among its female members 682 pilots, 290 navigators, and 223 air battle managers.

9.1.2 Scenario: A Bird's Eye View of Basic Training

At the time Reservist Candice Miscik decided to enlist, she had just graduated from high school and had no idea what she wanted to do next. She joined the Air Force to be able to travel and complete her education. "I was all over the place, and knew that I needed direction, and I needed discipline," she says. "My grandpa was in the Air Force, but no one else in my family was in the military. Even so, honestly, I knew it would be a good thing, so I just kind of went for it. And, I am so glad that I did, definitely," Miscik says, adding, "It is a part of me. I have no idea where I would be if I had not joined" (Miscik, 2016).

The California native, who remained on active duty until she became pregnant with her first child, has since served in the reserves for more than seven years. She describes what it was like to leave home for the first time, and go through basic training: "As soon as you arrive on the bus, everyone is in plain clothes, and they just start yelling at you. They do that on purpose," she says. "They try to break you down and then build you back up. But I just kept telling myself that it was all a mind game—no matter what you do, it is going to be wrong" (Miscik, 2016).

9.1.3 Conditions of Enlistment and Goals in Pursuing an Education

The hardest part for Miscik (2016) was being away from home for the first time. "I grew up in the same house, and joined when I was nineteen. I had never left home before. But, being away from my friends, you just learn to adjust," she says.

She was in an all-female "flight," which is a military term for a subgroup of a larger squadron. And she deployed with an "element," which is a squad of ten people. "While deployed, I was the only female on the squad from my base, and males outnumbered females."

Miscik describes one deployment situation where she served as a security forces apprentice, monitoring flight lines, entrance control points, and mobile patrols. "Every day we were sleep deprived; we would get maybe four or five hours a night. Then, when we woke up in the morning, we would have to do physical training that included push-ups, sit-ups, and long-distance running. I tried to work ten times harder to prove that I was equal and capable of the same level of responsibilities as the men," she states.

Miscik remembers another experience that quickly helped her to adapt to the Air Force's unique military culture. "It was scary to go into the chow hall to eat; you felt like a robot. You had to stand a certain way while you are sliding the tray down the line to get your meal." Toward the end of the line, Miscik described a group of training instructors who stationed themselves in and around the dessert station, which she called the "shark pit." "If you tried to grab a dessert, they would just go after you and yell at you." She says that the dining tables were set up in such a way that if one person stood up, everyone else had to stand at the same time.

The young recruit completed the Air Force's rigorous training program, but some others had a harder time. "I knew a girl in my class who couldn't even do one sit-up," she says. "Evidently, this girl had been given several chances to improve her performance, but was unsuccessful in meeting the physical demands."

Although Miscik does not actually know what happened to this fellow recruit, she offered a description of a military practice that is called being "washed out." If someone cannot pass the fitness tests, he or she can to told to start training all overall again. But if several more attempts produce the same results, that person could be "washed out" (Miscik, 2016).

9.2 THE AIR FORCE FROM AN "ACADEMIC" PERSPECTIVE

Today's Air Force officer has a 60 percent chance of having an "advanced or professional degree," and a 71 percent chance of being married. Officers are likely to be about thirty-five years old, but 37 percent are younger than twenty-six. Also, women account for 19 percent of the fighting forces and 20.3 percent of the officers, for a total female population of 59,292 ("Air Force Personnel Demographics," 2016).

Among the 812 Air Force Academy graduates in 2016, about one-quarter of the class is female. Additionally, 345 graduates plan to train as pilots, including 60 graduates who want to learn to operate drones and other remotely piloted aircraft that are used in counter-terrorism efforts (Lederman, 2016). To the galaxy and beyond!

Although Miscik does not plan to graduate this year, she is studying for her associate's degree in X-ray technology at a private brick-and-mortar school in California. Her initial plans to study at a local community college have changed for practical reasons. "I was on a wait list at one school for almost three years. There was a waiting list everywhere," she adds (Miscik, 2016).

9.2.1 Schools Likely to Attend and Factors Affecting Graduation Success

Moreover, when Miscik served on active duty, she tried online classes in hopes that this nontraditional approach to education could be successfully integrated into her already crowded schedule. Unfortunately, this plan did not work because being at a military post for eight to ten hours a day and trying to survive her classes was a virtual impossibility. Miscik also said that asynchronous classes were somewhat of a challenge and that she could not psychologically manage the courses unless they were "self paced" (Miscik, 2016).

She described one class that she dropped because the instructor, who was former military, e-mailed the class a precourse assignment before the scheduled term began. But Miscik was navigating her way through her professional responsibilities and did not know that this e-mail existed. She received little sympathy or support for her apparently untenable situation, so she decided to drop that course altogether.

Then, when she returned home, she no longer needed the flexibility offered by an online learning platform, and so she enrolled in a local community college. But the work was difficult, and when Miscik realized that she had to leave for reserve duty for two weeks, she decided to weigh her options. Ultimately, she dropped the class because she would be gone two weeks and felt that she woud not have enough time on her return to earn a passable grade.

Now, while taking care of her seven-year-old daughter, she continues to pursue her education, while also participating in regular military training two days a month and two full weeks a year. And although she still values the educational experience she is getting, she says that one instructor gave her twenty-four hours to make up any work that she had missed during her two-week training. That professor also deducted participation points for course activities and discussions that she could not complete during her absence (Miscik, 2016).

10

WHO IS THE COAST GUARD LEARNER?

10.1 WHO JOINS THIS BRANCH OF THE SERVICE AND WHY?

"Coasties" do more than just repetitively scour the ocean waters for lost or distressed boat enthusiasts. They actually keep a watchful eye on the maritime waters and arrest drug smugglers who are hiding their contraband aboard smaller seafaring boats and larger vessels. In addition, while grading papers may seem like a task that often zaps your energy until the wee hours of the morning, consider that members of the Coast Guard have been on duty twenty-four hours a day since 1790.

Somewhat paradoxically, not all Coast Guard service members are assigned to patrol coastal waters. Some guard waterways that are connected to regional or local ports of call (Lagan, 2014). Others perform such duties as enforcing laws on the open waters, breaking up ice blocks that can inhibit free travel, and working to preserve the environment.

Coast Guard Reserves are part-time service members who can be called into active duty in times of conflict, and the Coast Guard Auxiliary is comprised of volunteers who sometimes use their own boats or planes to teach public safety courses or lend a hand during Coast Guard emergencies ("A United States Coast Guard Life and Services Handbook: Sea Legs," n.d.).

The Coast Guard actually conducts rescues from the air and the open waters. A daily log of current activities performed by Coasties and auxiliary personnel who are hired to assist them include the following:

- Conduct 109 search and rescue cases
- Save ten lives
- Assist 192 people in distress
- Protect $2,791,841 in property
- Launch 396 small boat missions
- Launch 164 aircraft missions, logging 324 hours
- Board 144 vessels
- Seize 169 pounds of marijuana and 306 pounds of cocaine worth $9,589,000
- Intercept fourteen illegal migrants
- Board 100 large vessels for port safety checks
- Respond to twenty oil or hazardous chemical spills totaling 2,800 gallons
- Service 135 aids to navigation ("The Unique Role of the U.S. Coast Guard," 2016)

10.1.1 Testing the Waters: What It Takes to Join the Coast Guard

If you are not too fond of the water or envision a shark attacking you every time you set foot in the ocean, the Coast Guard is definitely not right for you. And the bottom line is, you have to know how to swim—well. In fact, to join the Coast Guard, you have to be able to jump from a 1.5-meter platform into a swimming pool and then complete 100 meters in less than five minutes. You will get dinged if you touch the bottom or the sides of the pool, and you cannot use goggles.

Another challenge is to tread water for five minutes without using a life jacket. Failure to pass either of these tests means that you will have to add a swim class to your regime, if, and when, you are able to meet the other qualification requirements. Once you are in, if you opt to join an elite unit called the "rescue swimmers," you will have to "hoist or free fall from a helicopter into dangerous seas to perform daring rescues" (www.gocoastguard.com). Back to grading papers; maybe academia is not that bad after all?

10.1.2 Coast Guard Protocol: Who Decides on the Mission?

This branch of the service is governed by the Department of Homeland Defense. But the president can, and frequently does, "transfer all assets of the Coast Guard to the Department of the Navy," during times of war and other conflict situations ("The Unique Role of the U.S. Coast Guard," 2016).

Among the list of famous people who served in or were associated with the Coast Guard are Humphrey Bogart, Lloyd Bridges and both of his actor sons, and famed news broadcaster Walter Cronkite. Even though Donald Duck wore just one suit in virtually every carton he ever made in print and film, he dressed up in a pirate suit to become a Coast Guard mascot during World War II ("Coast Guard History: Frequently Asked Questions," 2016).

11

WHO IS THE VETERAN LEARNER?

11.1 WHAT DEFINES THIS CATEGORY OF LEARNER?

According to a survey conducted by the American Council on Education (ACE), "sixty-two percent of veterans and military service members are the first in their family to attend college, compared to 43 percent of nonmilitary students." Veterans are also likely to enroll in four-year degree programs and to choose distance-learning options for convenience.

Yet the decision to pursue a degree versus the ability to earn one poses inherent challenges for many veteran learners. Getting credits they earned during military training to transfer to either a public or private university can be the greatest frustrations these students. Veterans are ready targets for profit-making institutions that deliver false promises about lucrative jobs and charge enormous fees for an education often not respected by private-sector employers. Frequent relocations related to their assignments can also cost the veteran the ability to meet state residency requirements for fee reductions or tuition assistance programs.

But even if a veteran successfully enrolls in school to better his or her life, he or she may still have to confront the risks associated with the time he or she spent in the service. Some of the reasons he or she may not be able to complete his coursework, aside from possible physical or emotional scars, is that he or she may not have the financial or emotional support during this transitional period of his or her life. These risk factors are significant if the student drops out of school because he or she may, and often does, end up homeless. About 1.4 million veterans are at risk for homelessness (Shaw, 2015).

11.1.1 Not the Type of Transition They Expected

On any given night, an estimated 47,725 veterans are homeless, and another 1.4 million are at risk of sleeping on the streets, according to the U.S. Department of Housing and Urban Development ("FAQ About Homeless Veterans," n.d.). The term *veteran* applies to anyone who has served in the U.S. Armed Forces and received an honorable discharge ("§1087vv. Definitions," n.d.). The concept of homelessness means that the veteran has no permanent residence or regular place to sleep at night ("Homeless Veterans Facts," n.d.).

Not only are veterans populating the nation's streets in increasing numbers, but women are also commonly seen among this group. According to the U.S. Department of Veterans Affairs, among the 22 million veterans identified as of 2015, about 9 percent are women (Statistics P. b., 2016). Unfortunately, it is much more common for female veterans to have developed a service-related disability and to live in poverty as well (Statistics P. b., "Profile of Veterans: 2014–Data from the American Community Survey," 2016).

11.1.2 Offering a Positive Alternative

One approach to keeping individuals who have served this country off the streets is to provide them with a quality education. That is, if they are still eligible, because once a person is discharged from the service, he or she is facing a timeclock, knowing that his or her GI bill benefits expire in a period of ten to fifteen years. That clock stops and starts again if the veteran chooses to reenlist and is deployed into active service (Howell, n.d.).

11.1.3 Goals that Deserve Recognition

Although many young men and women join the Armed Forces to fight their way out of poverty by earning enough money to afford a college education, veterans are more likely to end up sleeping on the streets than the general population. The same mental, physical, and financial issues that are directly linked to their active service duties can affect their potential to sit in your classroom and learn from you how to improve their futures.

The emotional and physical impacts of rape or other types of sexual traumas during a person's time in the service have only begun to surface recently; so it has yet to be established just how much these experiences affect veterans' ability to do well in the classroom.

11.2 OUR ROLE IN THE CLASSROOM AND ABILITY TO CHANGE LIVES

As college professors and part-time instructors, we may often feel that we are overworked and underpaid. But one motivation that appears to sustain us is the fact that we are making a difference in our students' lives. Knowledge can place students in a good position to enter the job market, once they have completed their degree.

We often feel like we have a special or unique capacity to reach out to our students to understand their specific learning needs. We also try to provide a learning environment that fosters diversity and inclusiveness. We want to be able to accomplish these same goals with our military students.

11.2.1 Reaching Out to Make a Difference

Still, unless we get to know these students and understand their desires, motivations, and experiences, our help may not be enough to reduce the veteran dropout rate, which stands close to 50 percent. Moreover, if there are statistics on how many college instructors—graduate and undergraduate—have actually served in one of the five branches of the military service, those number appear to be virtually impossible to find. Therefore, if we really do view ourselves as subject matter experts and resources for our students, what type of disservice are we doing to these individuals with whom we share no apparent commonalities?

Perhaps we need to recognize that our methods of transferring knowledge to our veteran learners just do not meet their needs. Hopefully, this handbook will help you to identify why your perceptions of who these students are and what they can accomplish may not be providing them with enough help to successfully transition back into the private sector, be rewarded for the academic milestones they are able to achieve, or to develop practical skills they need to get private-sector jobs.

11.3 FACTORS AFFECTING GRADUATION SUCCESS RATES

According to a Student Veterans of America (SVA) report, which investigated the results of Montgomery and Post–9/11 GI Bill benefits and success in college, 51.7 percent of veterans received a "postsecondary degree or certificate." This rate is comparable or greater than the graduate rates of "nontraditional" students. (These figures were released in association with the SVA's Million Records Project, which is designed to establish how well veterans are performing in college.)

Other information in the study reveals that veterans take between four and six years to complete their bachelor's degree and four years to get their associate's degree. Factors that sometimes delay completing their degrees include the decision to join the military and leave school, or to delay their education until after they have left the service. A third reason is that even though veteran students may have completed college courses before, during, and after their military service, some of the credits they earned do not transfer to the colleges or universities where they complete their degrees. Deployments can cause such delays too.

Although they may take more time to complete their education than the traditional college student, many of these veteran learners do pursue their graduate degrees.

The statistics gathered during this study were based on 788,915 records of "Montgomery and Post–9/11 GI Bill veteran education beneficiary records from 2002 to 2010, and U.S. student postsecondary enrollment and completion records collected by the NSC." This study population is roughly equivalent to 22 percent of student veterans who received GI Bill benefits during that time period.

11.3.1 Just the Facts

At the time of this publication, most sources contacted for information show that the success rates of veterans in colleges and universities are not carefully monitored or recorded. An explanation for this lack of data is that the funds for education are distributed by the Veterans Administration (VA) and not the U.S. Department of Education. The VA has prioritized tracking of funds over distribution of spending (McCann, 2014).

The main reason that most military students decide to pursue their degrees is to get a job in a field where their skills and knowledge will be in high demand. Those with associate's degrees often study liberal arts and sciences, business, homeland security, law enforcement, or health care. Student veterans who pursue their bachelor's degree focus on the fields of business, social sciences, homeland security, law enforcement, and firefighting, as well as computer and information sciences (Stewart, 2016).

11.4 FOLLOWING THE PAPER TRAIL

About 79 percent of veterans enroll in public schools and successfully get their degrees. The remainder study in private, nonprofit, or for-profit institutions. What these students are promised from the private universities versus what they actually receive have been the cause of both extensive federal investigations and harsh criticisms from President Obama. Investigations by the federal government, media, and States Attorneys General have forced many of these schools to shut down or to lose most of their students.

What has not been noted often enough is the marketing campaign of many for-profit schools target veterans who had ready access to their educational benefits. Other vulnerable target groups include single mothers in low-income categories. These tactics have led to the closing of such non-profit chains as Corinthian, which is the parent company of Everest, WyoTech, and Heald colleges. All of these colleges have been closed. When California Attorney General Kamala Harris launched her investigation of Corinthian's marketing tactics, she discovered these schools charged thousands of dollars, on the promise that a lucrative job would be waiting after graduation. Yet, the statistics revealed extremely low job-placement rates (Douglas-Gabriel, 2016).

The issue of private colleges even impacted the 2016 presidential campaign. Then–Republican nominee, Donald Trump, was able to delay several lawsuits filed by students who attended a private university he founded. Trump University is no longer in operation due to charges by students who alleged they were lied to about potential earnings after graduation. Trump University is closed, but the outcome of these lawsuits will not be decided until after the 2016 presidential election (Douglas-Gabriel, 2016).

11.5 SUCCESS RATES IN THE PRIVATE SECTOR AND TYPES OF CAREERS OFTEN PURSUED

The U.S. Bureau of Labor Statistics reports that 24 percent of post–9/11 veterans work for federal, state, or local governmental agencies, making the government the largest employer of this population. The federal government offers preference to veterans who have served on active duty over civilian job candidates. These benefits apply to applicants who qualify for both temporary and permanent positions

Veterans can also receive "appointments without competition" if they have received medals during active service, are disabled, or have finished their military contract within the past three years and received an honorable discharge ("Help Center," n.d.).

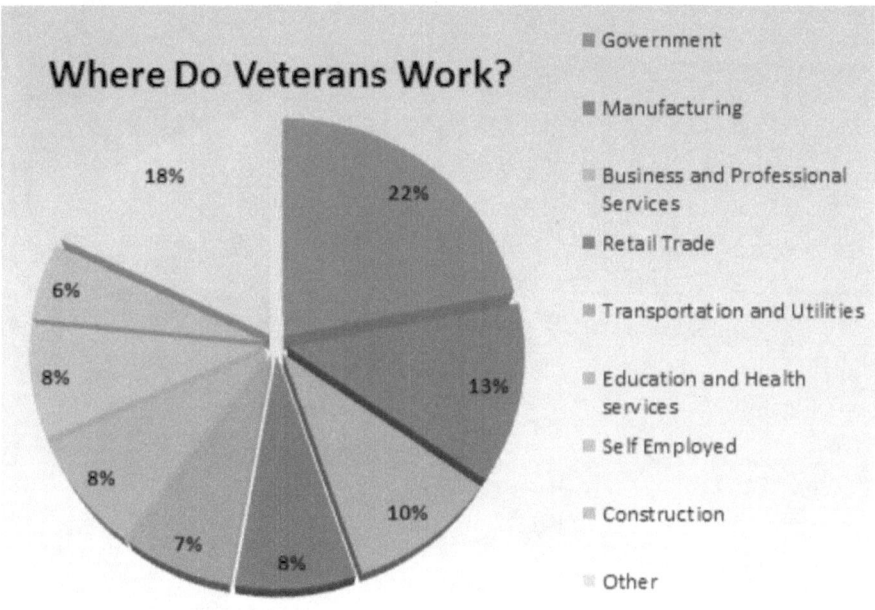

Figure 11.1. ("Jobs After the Military," 2016)

12

WHO ARE THE GOVERNMENT CONTRACTORS, RESERVISTS, AND MILITARY FAMILY MEMBER LEARNERS?

If you can't explain it simply, you don't understand it well enough.
–Albert Einstein

12.1 GOVERNMENT CONTRACTORS: A FORCE UNTO THEMSELVES

The military is a cohesive conglomeration of service members and people from the private sector who serve in essential interactive and supportive roles. But in discussing the battles being fought or won by members by the Armed Forces, we seldom consider how much gratitude we owe the people who perform jobs as civilian contractors. These professionals are hired for their knowledge and expertise, much in the same way that instructors are valued as subject matter experts (SMEs) ("Who are civilian contractors and what jobs do they perform overseas?" 2016).

12.1.1 Another Type of "Civilian"

So, if your student tells you that he or she works in an industry the government has contracted to serve alongside the military, what information is most useful to know about this person? Probably his or her role in helping to win wars is not unique, because many people who have ordinary jobs often end up serving on an overseas battlefield.

The phrase *civilian contractor* may not be familiar to you. These are people who work for private organizations and are paid to put their lives on the line to help stabilize or "re-stabilize" a conflict region. According to Micah Zenko, a senior fellow with the Center for Preventive Action at the Council on Foreign Relations, the ratio of private contractors to U.S. service members fighting in Afghanistan is about 3 to 1. Contractors also assist the CIA and participate in other intelligence operations that take place here and abroad.

But Zenko suggests that some of the individuals who serve in these contract roles tend to become the unknown victims of war. Thus, he charges that the federal government "refuses to provide consistent information about contractors," and "the news media neglect to bring attention to their role and sacrifices." Zenko further suggests that the "human costs" of war do not reflect the number of contractors who have been killed in conflicts, as opposed to their military counterparts (Zenko).

12.1.2 From Lectern to the Battlefield

As a college instructor, you have the opportunity to become a civilian contractor. These positions are part-time, and jobs are readily available. If you decide to pursue this career option, you could easily return to your teaching job once your military contract has ended. The compensation can range from $50,000 to $250,000 a year. The lure of tax-free earnings is probably not enough of an incentive to risk your life against well-armed enemies who have a much better sense of the geographical surroundings.

However, because the required time commitment can vary from a few months to several years, you will need to consider the potential financial or personal hardships that could result ("Who are civilian contractors and what jobs do they perform overseas?", 2016).

But, if you decide to temporarily exchange your keyboard for battle fatigues, you will not be alone. Contractors work for various sectors of private industy that include the following:

- Health care,
- Security,

- Engineering,
- Education,
- Construction,
- Transportation,
- Interpreters,
- Advising,
- Truck drivers,
- Food preparation,
- Information technology and telecommunications,
- Accounting,
- Mine removal,
- Agriculture,
- Sports and fitness,
- And, yes, even the military.

When you become a civilian contractor, you could be sent to such remote regions as Kosovo, Israel, Korea, or Liberia. Your skills and professional experiences determine where you will most be needed. For instance, if you have mechanical skills, you could wind up fixing tanks in Afghanistan. Or a nursing background could translate into treating the sick and injured in Iraq.

But the majority of military contractors actually work in security positions and are assigned to conflict regions. And forget about getting a regular night's sleep because you may have to handle twelve-hour shifts for six days in a row.

Could it be time to get back to grading?

12.2 RESERVISTS: MORE THAN ONE COMMITMENT

> The Reservist is twice the citizen.
> –Winston Churchill

One common misperception about people who join the military is that every member of the service is likely to be deployed or to engage in active fighting with enemy forces. Yet only about 15 percent of the professional jobs taught to members of the armed services are related to combat duty. The other 85 percent are in supportive roles. Examples include:

- disaster relief assistance,
- providing medical care or legal aid, and
- helping to build or rebuild in war-torn areas.

The military is likely to offer training for the same jobs found in the private sector ("Types of Military Service).

12.2.1 How to Distinguish a Reservist from an Active-Duty Learner

A division between the roles of an adjunct and full-time professor applies to the definitions of an active-duty service member versus a member of the Reserves. So someone on active duty has a full-time job with the military, whereas a reservist is usually only required to make a part-time commitment. Both undergo the same training, but a reservist can maintain a civilian job while fulfilling his or her military responsibilities.

Reservists also have the same choice as an active-duty service members, in that they can apply to become a member of all service branches. When they sign the contract, it stipulates that their reservist status can change to active-duty if their skills are needed in a conflict zone, but they are usually required to train one weekend a month and complete field exercises semi-annually.

12.2.2 Military Family Members: Playing a Supportive Role

> The true soldier fights not because he is afraid of what is in front of him, but because he loves what is behind him.
> –G. K. Chesterton, English writer, poet, and philosopher

For the military spouse, making friends is easier than getting a degree, according to Joyce Wessel Raezer, executive director of the National Military Family Association. Her organization evolved from a small group of determined military spouses in Annapolis, Maryland, who bonded together to ask Congress for legislative reforms that would entitle them to receive military benefits if their spouses were deceased. Thanks in part to their efforts, service members can transfer benefits to their spouse or children if they have been in the service for six years and commit to more.

Wessel Raezer's (2016) nonprofit organization continues to advocate for military families, even offering a military spouse scholarship program. "Our mission is to speak up for military families and do what we can, either through or advocacy, to keep military families strong."

Funded entirely by corporate foundation and individual donors, the organization received 7,500 applicants for its 2015 Spouse Scholarship program. Out of the applicant pool, about 600 people were awarded grants in the average range of $1,000. "We have received stories from thousands and thousands of spouses describing what types of challenges they face on their educational journey," Wessel Raezer (2016) said. "And their issues are very different from veterans going back to school, or children going back to school."

There is no such thing as a stereotypical military spouse, Wessel Raezer says. Some are recent high school graduates, and others have been out of school for a long time. They usually do not have a network to help them learn how to complete college applications or to select a course list once they get into a school. So, they have to figure out for themselves what types of colleges to attend, what courses to take, and what majors will enable them to be qualified for their careers.

"Because the education landscape nationally has changed, you have a lot more kinds of educational offerings, so how does someone know what the best educational setting is for them, in order to achieve the goals they have set for themselves," Wessel Raezer (2016) says.

According to Wessel Raezer, a lot of military spouses are not enrolled in traditional four-year schools. "While some of the younger ones can say they are going to make the commitment to go to school full time, others do not have that option. They prefer to enroll in a community college or online school, which means their educational journey is going to take a lot longer" (Wessel Raezer, 2016).

Even if the military spouse does get into the college of his or her choice, he or she may not be able to complete his or her education at that same institution once a deployment occurs.

12.2.3 A Long Way from Home

"On average, a military family moves every 2.9 years," Wessel Raezer (2016) says. They may also be forced to quit jobs, which can lead to serious financial problems if the family is transferred to a high-cost area.

Additional frustrations can be caused by the realization that foregoing their educations will delay the opportunities to provide better financial support for their families.

"In general, research has shown that military spouses are more likely to be unemployed than their civilian peers," Wessel Raezer says. "The unemployment rate for military spouses is 25 percent, according to the Department of Defense. There are several research studies that show military spouses are significantly under-employed when compared to their civilian-age and education peers" (Wessel Raezer, 2016).

But deployments can, and do, affect the entire family. Imagine that someone you love deeply spends several years with you, and then, suddenly, he leaves for six months to six years at a time. And the only contact you have with him or her is periodic visits home, which may only last for a few days or weeks. Not an easy situation to contemplate. The decision to become a service member impacts the entire family on deep emotional, physical, financial, and psychological levels.

Among the most difficult struggles that military families face is the ability to maintain a regular routine. According to an essay published by Rand, when a family member is deployed, related stresses and pressures may continue to build up over time (Irving, 2016). If the service member deploys, the remaining spouse is now confronted with the cost of education and also possibly the cost of child care. If he or she cannot afford both, he or she may have to delay education until the service member comes back. But transfer orders can come in again as well.

12.2.4 From a Child's Perspective

The child of service members may have additional issues to face when he or she tries get into college. If the parent has made a career of serving in the military, the child may have been forced to repeatedly change schools. Moreover, because they have to change schools so frequently, chances are they have never been able to serve on student councils or in other types of roles that can distinguish their application from other applicants. Now, when they are filling out college applications, they know that their situation is one that is probably not familiar to those individuals who will be reviewing the application.

But the experiences they have had, particularly if they have been forced to act as babysitter for an absentee parent or a caregiver for a wounded service member, will probably not impress the college selection committee. Neither will the level of resilience they have been able to display while the family moved around or their ability to learn different educational styles at each school while making new friends. These skills are as intangible as the level of maturity they have displayed in readily accepting their role in their families.

12.3 IS ACKNOWLEDGMENT IMPORTANT?

If you do not have access to resources to help your military student family members, you are not alone. Most information about how deployments affect success in higher education is focused on service members and veterans, not family members. To understand how well military families do in an undergraduate or graduate environment, it is necessary to chart that individual's progress at any college or university where courses have been completed. "There is no a requirement by the Department of Education that universities require veterans to report their status when they enroll at a university. The university will know if students' requests to use their GI benefits, but most universities do not track the academic performance of veterans separately from other students."

What can be determined, however, are the amount of times a child has transferred to a new school district. For younger children, this means getting used to a new school district and making a whole new set of friends. But for spouses, or children who are enrolled in college, frequent moves can cause setbacks in getting degrees, if the credits do not transfer or certain college courses are not offered in a new school.

Tuition fees can be lost if the move occurs mid-term or semester, and some students can risk flunking classes if their instructor does not allow them to drop the course or take an incomplete. If the new college is located in a district where classrooms are filled to capacity, a student may have to wait weeks or months before continuing his or her degree (The White House—President Barack Obama, n.d.).

Both President and Michelle Obama worked on initiatives to improve the educational experiences of military learners Among the improvements made include a monitoring system to identify how may many students who have used post–9/11 GI Bill since 2009 have completed their degrees at four-year institutions. Based on the data that has already been collected, MacDermid Wadsworth (2016) says that those who benefit from the post–9/11 GI Bill may not take more semesters to graduate, "but it may take them more calendar time."

There was a time when the Ivy Leagues were going to have ROTCs on campuses. There are veteran students in Ivy League universities today. For some of these colleges, having a bright veteran in your classroom is almost a status symbol.

12.3.1 An Instructor's Role

You may have military family members in your classroom and not even know it. Wessel Raezer (2016) states that military spouses in any education environment are going to be much more invisible than a veteran would be. They don't have the ball cap; they don't have the uniform. If you are educating adult learners, they are just one of many. There is nothing stamped on their forehead that says "military spouses."

What is equally invisible is their motivation to learn, which is quite substantial, according to Wessel Raezer. Because the majority of these learners are not receiving federal aid, they want to make sure that they are getting a quality education in return for the amount they are spending on tuition and related class expenses (Wessel Raezer, 2016).

12.3.2 What to Do If Problems Arise

> It is better to light a candle than curse the darkness.
> –Eleanor Roosevelt

"If a student is not performing well in our class, whether they are trying, or even if they are not, we have an obligation to help them," MacDermid Wadsworth (2016) adds. "Our responsibility is to focus on the performance, and not the reasons why they are having troubles in our classroom." She uses an analogy about another group that is commonly recognized under the umbrella of diversity to explain her meaning. "If someone has moved twelve times, and that is interfering with their performance, then our job is to help them with their *performance*. It is not really our job to determine why they are having trouble, but to assist them if they are."

Finally, MacDermid Wadsworth points out that military family members can add a great deal to the classroom experience because they may have traveled globally and may contribute in interesting ways to class discussions (MacDermid Wadsworth, 2016).

13

DEFINING BASIC TYPES OF MEDICAL, PHYSICAL, AND PSYCHOLOGICAL CONDITIONS THAT CAN AND DO IMPACT MILITARY LEARNERS

The soldier above all others prays for peace, for it is the soldier who must suffer and bear the deepest wounds and scars of war.
–Gen. Douglas MacArthur

13.1 NO ADVICE IS BEING OFFERED

A person is able to enter the military because he or she is physically fit and appears psychologically stable. In addition, he or she can be proud to be chosen, because only about 20 percent of people in this country who are between the ages of seventeen and twenty-four can actually qualify to enlist. So, for those of you who teach in brick-and-mortar classrooms, take a brief moment to glance around the room at your students before you begin your next lecture.

Do you see individuals with piercings, tattoos, or elongated earlobes? Well, they are not eligible to join the military. And if they take medication for hyperactivity, they are ineligible, too. But the biggest factors preventing young people from entering the service is they cannot meet the weight requirements. Maj. Gen. Allen Batschelet, commander of the U.S. Army Recruiting Command, stated in a *Business Insider* article that the problem is only getting worse ("Here's why most Americans can't join the military," 2015).

What happens to those individuals who do make the cut and complete their term of service? Do they arrive back home in the same condition that they were in during basic training? Not always. During their term of service, they may have had experiences that left them physically, emotionally, or psychologically scarred for the rest of their lives. Twenty-three percent of more than 8,500 of Gulf War and post–9/11 veterans, active-duty service members, members of the National Guard and Reserves, and military-connected dependents, said that "issues related to wellness and/or disability "posed challenges to completing their degrees, according to a study conducted by researchers at Syracuse University's Institute for Veterans and Military Families (Zoli, Maury, & Fay, 2015).

That is not to say all military veterans leave the service with debilitating illnesses. In fact, "most service members are not wounded . . . and have no long-lasting health problems" (Clever & Segal, 2013).

However, this section addresses some of the injuries and illnesses that can impact service members and affect their ability to perform well in your classroom. Please keep in mind as you read this chapter that the information provided is not intended to offer medical advice or to help you assess military students' learning capacity. What it might offer you, instead, is a look at the obstacles some students face, and help you become a better resource for these learners.

13.1.1 Acronym for an Illness

> Your illness does not define you, your strength and courage does.
> –Anonymous

Today, there are almost as many acronyms used by physicians to describe illnesses as there are weaponry terms identified with abbreviations in the military stylebook, *The Tongue and Quill*. But one of the most important for you to know about if you are working with military students is *post-traumatic stress disorder* or PTSD (U.S. Dept. of Veterans Affairs, 2016).

PTSD is a term that is commonly known and describes injuries that may or may not have physical signs or symptoms. But this complex condition impacts the person's ability to function and may make a student reluctant to spend time in your classroom.

PTSD could have triggering events that occurred months, if not years, ago. Often a person who has been in a battle situation, has been injured, or has seen a fellow soldier become wounded or, is severely traumatized, but cannot necessarily respond to these experiences immediately. But when emotions do surface, the person can then begin to evidence signs of PTSD.

13.2 THE TRAUMA OF SEXUAL HARASSMENT

PTSD symptoms can also occur in victims of *military sexual trauma* or MST. MST includes incidents of sexual assault or repeated threatening sexual harassment that occur in the military. Symptoms of MST that affect the student's classroom performance include frequent and unexplained absences, inability to interact with peers, lack of participation in group activities, and behaviors associated with PTSD.

Although both men and women have reported being victims of MST, more incidents appear to occur among women. For instance, one in four female veterans who have sought medical services through the VA said she had experienced MST (U.S. Department of Veterans Affairs, 2015). Such incidents can occur during peacetime, training, or war ("Mental Health Effects of Serving in Afghanistan and Iraq," 2015).

Symptoms of MST might begin with nightmares or trouble sleeping. Flashbacks and painful memories may surface unexpectedly as well. Those memories can trigger avoidance behaviors that result in the student being perpetually late for your class or chronically absent without contacting you to offer an excuse.

Although military learners may not choose to divulge their psychological condition to you, they may display PTSD symptoms in the classroom anyway. What you could observe is that they appear to be extremely anxious and hyper-alert to their surroundings. You may interpret their actions as a lack of interest in the subject you are teaching or as an unwillingness to participate in your class. In fact, their motivation may actually be related to avoiding feelings of fear, guilt, or shame. If their condition has escalated to the point that they feel unable to repress memories of whatever trauma they have experienced, they could exhibit or begin internalizing feelings of severe depression ("Mental Health Effects of Serving in Afghanistan and Iraq," 2015).

13.3 SERVICE-RELATED INJURIES YOU MAY NOT BE ABLE TO DETECT

Some service members sustain *traumatic brain injury* or TBI, which is an injury to the brain that is caused by a blow or other physical force. Although the impact of sustaining such an injury may only be temporary, if the condition persists, symptoms that can result include frequent headaches, memory impairment, poor concentration levels, inability to pay attention, and changes in mood.

Individuals who have already had a concussion or who have a history of substance abuse are also more prone to develop TBI. Consequently, service members can develop TBI and never have been deployed, or they could sustain this type of injury during a combat situation. Bullet fire or fragments, rollover crashes, falls, vigorous sporting activities, and assaults can also result in TBI.

Yet not enough is known about TBI to pinpoint which symptoms will occur for each individual or to accurately predict just how long this condition will last. However symptoms can persist or even worsen, especially if injury reoccurs ("TBI Basics," 2016).

13.4 HOW DO THESE CONDITIONS AFFECT SCHOOL PERFORMANCE?

The range and depth of TBI symptoms can actually vary from mild to severe. For instance, students who suffer from mild TBI symptoms may have difficulty with maintaining their sense of balance. They may experience headaches, problems with vision, or appear to be somewhat disoriented, and can have trouble remembering information from lecture or text materials. In addition, they may have seizures and difficulty speaking. But if they have severe TBI symptoms, they can also become insensitive to changes in sound, temperature, smell, touch, and taste. Moreover, they could have trouble sleeping, lose motivation, and develop irritability, aggressive , or depressive behaviors ("Mild TBI Symptoms").

Because of their condition, they can have difficulty hearing lectures or discussions, especially when there is background noise or multiple conversations going on all at once. Dr. Katherine L. Mitchell, former medical director at Phoenix VA Medical Center Post-Deployment Clinic and current specialty care medicine lead for the Veterans Integrated Service Network Office 22, recommends making an announcement like the following at the beginning of the term: "I would ask that all students keep background noise to a minimum and avoid speaking at the same time as another student. If anyone has difficulty with hearing the lecture or the discussion, please let me know so we can make accommodations" (Mitchell 2016).

Mitchell says the symptoms of TBI can overlap with PSTD. And even though no physical signs of either condition may be visible to you, the military student's academic performance can nonetheless be compromised.

But Mitchell, who is a strong proponent of high-quality health care for veterans and for the implementation of resources that will increase the chances of veteran reintegration into the civilian world, cautions against painting with too broad a brushstroke. Many veterans who suffer PTSD, TBI, or MST have adopted coping skills and may be fully functional in all areas of their lives.

"Veterans with TBI or other chronic conditions have variable strengths and needs due to invisible effects of military service. So I would avoid stereotyping these students into a single category, and to instead maintain an awareness of the challenges these individuals face due to invisible physical effects of military service" (Mitchell, 2016).

13.5 WHAT CAN YOU DO TO HELP?

> No one is useless in this world
> Who lightens the burden of another.
> –Charles Dickens

As a professor, your role is not to "fix" the problem or to find a cure. Displaying sensitivity to military learners means trying to integrate them into the classroom through the use of appropriate accommodations. They do not want to be singled out in front of his or her classmates because of their medical diagnoses or need for assistance in dealing with service-related injuries.

Therefore, Mitchell (2016) suggests you can make the following remarks on the first day of class, so that your military students will feel more comfortable.

- Suggestion 1: "If there is any assignment that is too sensitive in nature to complete, please let me know and we can discuss an alternative."
- Action 1: Allow students to take a test in a quiet room if ambient noises pose significant distractions.
- Suggestion 2: "Some students require breaks during class time or need to leave early. If you require such accommodations, please notify me privately, so we can make appropriate arrangements."
- Action 2: Give students additional time for testing if they have impaired memory, recall, or difficulties concentrating.
- Suggestion 3: "If there is anyone who will need to be absent due to medical appointments, please let me know. I do not need to know the nature of the medical appointment. Just let me know what time and date you will be unable to attend, and I will not deduct points."
- Action 3: Provide your lecture notes in advance, if students have problems with memory, retention, or concentration.

Mitchell also recommends that you contact the disability resource center on your campus to learn what accommodations are available to all students with learning disabilities. Be aware of the potential advantages these accommodations offer to your students and what formal accommodations that are legally required to be implemented have been approved by your school. Encourage students to go to their counselors and get more information about formal accommodations to determine if these services may benefit them.

13.6 WHEN ANGER IS AN ISSUE

Teaching is obviously a challenging occupation. And as you may or may not have learned by now, some of the situations you could face are unpredictable. For instance, aggressive behavior is identified as one possible behavioral outcome of either TBI or PTSD. Alcohol or drug use, as well as severe depression, are factors which can contribute to these outcomes (Hinds, 2016). Unfortunately, the use of drugs or alcohol can cause these PTSD symptoms to intensify (U.S. Department of Veterans Affairs, 2015).

If your military learners evidence signs of irritation or aggression, what can you do? First of all, recognize that they may not be aware that they are exhibiting inappropriate behavior so challenging them could actually cause the situation to escalate. But if you are unsure about your own safety, then placing distance between you and the student is probably a good idea. Moreover, if you speak to the student in a calm tone of voice and try to understand their issues or concerns, you may help to ease tensions.

13.7 ADJUSTING TO PHYSICAL INJURIES

It is hard to say whether students have a harder time adjusting to the physical or emotional traumas they have experienced during their term of service. If their injuries are obvious, such as blindness or the amputation of a limb, the issues they experience in an educational environment tend to be quite different. For instance, if they had a leg amputated, they may have trouble walking around the campus or to and from classes. And if surgery occurred recently, they may not have adjusted to using crutches or other assistive devices, such as a wheelchair or a knee brace, that allow them to get around.

Other injuries involving chronic pain are not as obvious, yet they still require adjustments in the learning environment. These needs will vary, depending on the student and the effects of their injuries. One possible accommodation for students who have mobility issues is to allow them to leave five minutes before the class ends (Mitchell, 2016).

13.8 A VETERAN'S CHALLENGES

People who have served in the military will not walk into your class and announce their previous profession. Nor do they ask you to feel sorry for them if they are having trouble adjusting to civilian life. So you may not know or recognize that they are experiencing difficulties in trying to adapt to the culture of an academic environment.

To try to understand the situation veterans face in your classroom if they were deployed for any extended period of time, consider that you have been offered a one-year sabbatical, and that the university that has issued the invitation to teach is halfway around the world. This opportunity may sound great to you at first because you will have a chance to travel—all expenses paid—and you will be gaining experience that can help to advance your career. But after giving this idea careful consideration, you start to realize that accepting this invitation means leaving your family, friends, and colleagues behind, as well as figuring out how to pay your bills while you are away.

Even if military learners were never deployed during their time in the service, they may still be apprehensive about being in a classroom with much younger classmates who do not share their experiences. And they may also feel like they do not have anyone to help them cope with these stressors. Such factors can interfere with their concentration abilities and may be exacerbated by the length of time since they have been inside a nonmilitary classroom. If they believe that your teaching style is not as highly structured as the military's, or that your expectations of them are not clearly spelled out, they may have an even more difficult time making the adjustment. Whether or not they have faced battle situations, their learning abilities could still be affected by transitioning back to civilian life, the adverse effects of using medications, or health-related concerns (Mitchell, 2016).

13.8.1 The Trials of Returning Home

The same issues exist when veterans come home after completing their military service. They may have been separated from their family for a long time and are now leaving behind a lifestyle that represents comfort and familiarity. They may also feel that no one in their newly reconnected home environment can understand the experiences they have had. Moreover, in their absence, someone else in the family may have assumed their role, and now they have to adjust to resuming those responsibilities again.

If they were transferred during their military service, they had help to make the transition. But now that kind of assistance is gone, and members of their family are probably significantly older than when they first enlisted. So they have to cope with adjusting to attitudes and behaviors that are no longer familiar. And their spouses and children are also trying to familiarize themselves with a parent who has changed substantially during their absence.

13.8.2 Making New Adjustments

If they are pursuing a degree, they are probably working to support their family. But they may not know how to write a resume if they entered the military right after high school or were never previously employed in the private sector. They could also be afraid that their skills are outdated, and worry that they will not be able to earn enough money to pay their expenses ("Fact Sheet: Veteran Homelessness, Questions and Answers on Homelessness Policy and Research," 2015).

Once veterans return to work, they may start to believe their job is at risk because their skills have become outdated. Reservists and National Guards members who have been temporarily deployed could be required to return to work just a few days after they return home, giving them little time to make the transition.

Some of the adjustments the veteran must make in the workforce will apply to your classroom as well. For instance, the culture and style of communication among traditional students may be difficult for military learners to easily comprehend because they have learned to be clear, direct, and brief in their communications. They may not understand some students' reluctance to complete tasks in a group situation because they have been taught that they are not fulfilling their duties unless they have completed an assigned task.

They may also not understand students with laidback attitudes, or those prioritize their own academic needs above their desire to get along with other class members. Veterans have learned that cooperation is essential to preserve their own lives as well as the lives of those serving with them ("Mental Health Services: Common Challenges & How to Help, Common Challenges During Readjustment," n.d.).

When military students have trouble adjusting to civilian life, they may be coping with different types of traumatic issues. Or, if they have experienced an illness or injury while deployed, they may not work well in a classroom structure that is loose and informal because they have had every move planned out for them for such a long time.

If they develop feelings of anxiety or hopelessness, they may become severely depressed. Over time, anxiety and depression can lead to even more severe consequences, such as drug abuse, alcoholism, involvement in criminal activity, homelessness, or even suicide. Sexual assault can also lead to similar consequences (Sales, 2015).

13.9 HOW MUCH ARE YOU EXPECTED TO KNOW?

> The secret in education lies in respecting the students.
> –Ralph Waldo Emerson

If you have never served, you will probably not recognize the nonverbal messages your students may be sending to you about their level of comfort or discomfort in the classroom. And you are not required to know such information either. But you definitely do need to respond to the physical and psychological injuries that military students have sustained. Even if your roster does not tell you whether you have military students, you can provide assistance without that knowledge.

Keep in mind that many veterans experience chronic pain because they were constantly required to carry heavy equipment around, go on long and difficult marches, and jump off vehicles. These types of actions then lead to premature joint damage that causes pain. So they could have chronic trouble with pain in their lower back, knees, and shoulders, all of which could contribute to their inability to stay seated in one spot for a long period of time.

If students do divulge difficulty with a physical, emotional, or learning issue, you can tell them you are grateful they have chosen to share this information with you. Ask the student if an accommodation can be provided that can help them to cope with the issue and succeed in your classroom.

13.10 Does Acknowledgment Help? Respecting FERPA Laws and Guidelines

In this section, you will read about one of the most important resources you have to assist you in guiding your students toward more effective outcomes in the classroom. That resource is *you*. Thus, although students may have specific identified needs that set them apart in some ways from your more traditional students, you are the instructor and have to decide how you will approach them, from the standpoint of trying to best facilitate learning needs.

So whether you are a first-year instructor or a seasoned professor who is just encountering military students for the first time, what you want to decide is how you can acknowledge that your students' battle experiences may be affecting their academic potential. Obviously not an easy decision for anyone to make, particularly if you have never set foot on a military base in your life. How do you decide what is the best approach to take?

Dr. Linda DiDesidero is director of the Leadership Communications Skills Center at Marine Corps University in Quantico, Virginia. She teaches graduate-level courses in writing and speaking as well as in leadership communication. Fifty percent of the students who attend the Marine Corps University are Marine Corps officers, and the other 50 percent are from the "sister services," or governmental agencies, such as the U.S. Department of Homeland Security. A smaller percentage of the latter group is officers from diverse global regions. Moreover, an even smaller representation of the total student population is female officers, or the equivalent of about 5 percent.

Probably the most useful advice DiDesidero has to offer could also be a bit surprising as well. She says that you should get to know your students and provide them with one-on-one feedback if the need arises. Her opinions about why this approach works best could shatter any stereotypical images you may have about the cold and somber attitudes of most military personnel. According to DiDesidero (2016), contrary to popular belief, the military is a very caring organization. As a caveat, she adds that the Marines may indeed be the most caring service branch of all. "Officers view themselves as teachers, and so it is very important for them to take care of the men and the women who serve among their ranks, and the families of these service members as well."

She adds that counseling is an activity commonly used from the time that individuals enter the service, up until they become officers and take over the counseling role themselves. This early phase of their training is referred to as their *professional military education* or PME. The reason they are counseled by their supervising officers is to assist them in setting goals, establishing realistic measurement standards for their own achievements, and discussing performance issues that could stand in the way of their advancement. During these regular counseling sessions, they also review the results of physical fitness training scores.

What DiDesidero (2016) suggests is to simply use the same type of learning strategy that the military students have become accustomed to in the service. If you make yourself available to them by setting up times to meet after class or during regular office hours, you will have a much better chance of earning their trust and being able to effectively successfully guide them during the learning process. "If faculty members make this opportunity available to their military students, it is probably something they will take advantage of, because they are used to being mentored," Dr. DiDesidero says. "They see all subject matter experts as people who has something to offer them."

DiDesidero also reinforces that you never make assumptions about your military learners. Consider that whether or not they have been engaged in combat, they could still be grappling with issues, like PTSD, developed during their service. Even though federal laws are in place to protect the student's right to privacy, she said it is still a "good teaching principle to get to know your students and their potential needs as best as you can." This advice applies to instructors who teach online and in a brick-and-mortar classroom.

And if students do have a condition that impacts their ability to function in the classroom, the teacher generally receives notification of such issues during the first weeks of class or students advise their instructor during that same time frame. Many schools also have policies regarding reasonable accommodations that can be provided to students, when and if the need arises (DiDesidero, 2016). For new faculty members, it is important to acquaint yourself with the guidelines of the Family Educational Rights and Privacy Act (FERPA).

According to the U.S. Department of Education web site, FERPA is a federal law "that protects the privacy of student education records. The law applies to all schools that receive funds under an applicable program of the U.S. Department of Education" (U.S. Department of Education, 2015).

But FERPA laws do not prevent you from making sure your military students know who on campus should be notified of their condition and how they can get access to any necessary accommodations. Similarly, you need to know if your students are affected by PTSD or TBI, so you can make an informed analysis of their behavior if they decide to sit in the back of the classroom facing the wall. Realizing that this behavior is not directed at you and that they are not necessarily displaying a lack of interest in the subject matter you are teaching will help you to identify that they are just trying to cope.

Finally, DiDesidero suggests educating yourself about what these learners have experienced and how the issues they are now facing affect their learning. High on the list of recommended resources are books and articles written from the perspective of service members who have returned home with conditions similar to those experienced by students in your class.

Part of the reason to arm yourself with knowledge is because most faculty members do not have a "broad cultural knowledge of what it means to be a military learner." DiDesidero (2016) says this situation relates to the presence of an all-volunteer military, which can create a division between those who choose to serve and those who do not.

14

THE PAST, PRESENT, AND FUTURE OF MILITARY EDUCATION: WHAT THE EXPERTS HAVE TO SAY

Tell me, I forget; teach me, I remember; involve me, I learn.
–Benjamin Franklin

14.1 ASSESSING THE BEST APPROACH TO PROVIDING QUALITY EDUCATION

The term *education* represents a broad spectrum of approaches to learning. But within the pages of this handbook, the concept of education has been narrowed significantly to focus almost exclusively on the needs of military learners. Because you are reading the final chapter, you may still have some questions about why you should consider the needs of these students separately from the needs of your more traditional learners.

Within the past decade, an estimated $68 billion has been spent on educating more than 1.6 million students. A few of these students could be occupying your classroom seats right now, but consider that eligible beneficiaries have fifteen years from their last period of active duty to use their post–9/11 GI Bill (Coy, 2016).

Reviewing this chapter, you will find historical references to attitudes, opinions, and information about how the education of military students has evolved over the past decade, what is currently viewed as acceptable practice, and whether future predictions could lead to major changes in transferring knowledge to this particular student population. This information is designed to help you make informed decisions when you apply some of the techniques defined in this text and to help you understand what the experts believe are the most significant or pressing issues to consider in the process.

Assessing the best approach to providing a quality educational experience to military learners can help you establish an equal playing field for *all* of the students whose names appear on your roster. Because these names may not have been included in college enrollment figures for the past four to twenty years, they will be relying on you, to some degree, to help them acclimate.

14.1.1 Meet the Experts

Research conducted for this handbook illustrated the apparent gaps in substantial information that can help you to effectively guide your military students toward successful outcomes. Moreover, the opinions of those who have served and those who work in leadership roles within the educational system often appear to represent opposite sides of the spectrum. This final chapter is dedicated to letting the experts offer their opinions of what the best practices are in the classroom and how to optimize the integration of military learners into your teaching pedagogy.

- **Curtis L. Coy**: Deputy Under Secretary for Economic Opportunity, Department of Veterans Affairs
- **Marla Geha**: Professor of Astronomy and Physics at Yale University; participated in the Warrior-Scholar Project
- **Michael William Marks**: Professor of Practice in Psychology/Director Supportive Education for Returning Veterans - SUMC VETS Center, University of Arizona
- **Alexander Baldwin McCoy**: Political Science Student at Columbia and former Marine Sergeant
- **Trevor Pontifex**: Pomona College geology major and former Marine Sergeant. His letter to the editor appeared in the *New York Times* on Sept. 12, 2016, under the headline, "Admit Editors to Elite Colleges."
- **Joyce Wessel Raezer**: Executive Director of the National Military Family Association.

- **Brian Ragunan**: Program Coordinator of Vets/Services for Transfer and Reentry Students (STARS) at University of California, Santa Cruz
- **Logan Leslie**: U.S. Army Special Forces Veteran who is now serving in the Special Forces of the National Guard. Attending the JD/MBA program at Harvard University

The experts who have consented to offer their opinions were individually chosen based on their level of knowledge and expertise in education, military service, student experiences and needs, or the reported societal treatment of learners who serve or have served in the U.S. Armed Forces.

Perhaps among all of the separate divisions of this text, this final chapter allows the greatest opportunity for you to reflect on your own ideas and opinions and to decide which of these experts can help you to design your course structure and classroom materials. Finally, each person was provided with the same questions, but was only asked to address those items he or she felt most comfortable answering.

14.2 THE STATE OF MILITARY EDUCATION TEN YEARS AGO

14.2.1 Issue One: Landscape of Target Marketing by Private Schools

Probably one of the greatest blemishes on postsecondary education that has occurred in recent years is the marketing campaigns orchestrated by some private, profit-making schools to attract federal dollars from military students. Was that trend a sign that our educational system was somehow "dumbing down," in an attempt to put profit before educational rigor? Alexander Baldwin McCoy says no. In his opinion, the real reason schools were allowed to boost their bottom line through GI bill funds is because of an apparent gap in federal laws that govern how these institutions may operate. He explains,

> I think there is a major federal legal loophole in something called the "90/10 rule," which establishes a strong predatory incentive for these for-profit colleges to enroll active duty and veteran students. Although

this rule was actually an attempt to regulate these institutions, the law allowed for these schools to obtain 10 percent of their revenue from students who receive military assistance and educational benefits, and the other 90 percent could come from student aid. There is proposed legislation changing the 90/10 to include GI Bill and Tuition Assistance.

Unfortunately, the successful lobbying efforts of these schools meant that, instead of needing to attract paying customers, all they had to do was to attract military students to make up for the remaining 10 percent (McCoy, 2016).

Dr. Michael William Marks describes what circumstances led to the proliferation of private schools. During the past decade, and in particular after 9/11, more veterans started to enroll in college campuses. Some had just returned from tours of duty in either Iraq or Afghanistan, and that was when, as Marks describes it, the "whole rodeo started" (Marks, 2016). "Ten years ago, we were right in the middle of two wars, and veteran learners were just more visible," agrees Brian Ragunan (2016).

14.2.2 Issue Two: Being Denied Proper Recognition

Perhaps one question you are asking yourself as you read through this handbook is, are guidelines really needed? After all, we have had a military presence on most college campuses since our country's inception, so why should we, as teachers, have to learn to be more aware of how we treat our military students?

According to Dr. Marks, perhaps the answer lies not in the rapid influx of students to college campuses within the past decade, but in the fact that their presence was neither recognized nor appreciated during that era in our nation's history. Vestiges of anger against the U.S. participation in the Vietnam War led to some instructors' biased views of military learners.

But Marks, who used to be a hardcore anti-war activist before becoming a director of a counseling program for veterans, explains that the people who fought in Vietnam should not have been made society's whipping posts for actions this country and its leaders perpetrated. "I had friends who went to Vietnam and came back with their legs missing. So, I opposed the war; not the people who went there, because for everyone that didn't go, somebody else went in their place" (Marks, 2016).

14.2.3 Issue Three: Fear of Independent Thought

You cannot train people to be fighters unless you are able to get them to focus on a singular mission. However, in doing so, you are also organizing people into groups that prioritize the values of respect of authority and obedience to a cause above the expression of their own original thoughts and ideas. Asking that same group to enter a college or graduate school classroom, where questions of existence are raised or global warming issues are being examined, may be like asking military learners to accurately describe themselves while standing in front of a carnival mirror.

Marks states that the military requires its service members to prioritize the mission above all else: "If we wanted you to have an independent thought, we would have issued you one." Consequently, when the veteran decides to enter the world of academia, "the whole culture is flipped, because they want you to question everything" (Marks, 2016).

14.2.4 Issue Four: Lack of Understanding

Ten years ago, another issue that military learners often confronted was that, even when their ranks were acknowledged by administrators and programs were set up on their behalf, the organizers of such efforts had no real understanding of who these individuals were or how their needs could be met. So, Marks adds, while "people with good intentions" set up programs to help military learners succeed in college, they did so without considering these students' experiences or inviting their input. Essentially, the administrators probably told the learners what they needed to know and may have often discounted military students' abilities to enrich the culture of the academic environment (Marks, 2016).

Brian Ragunan agrees: "I don't believe that professors had the same concept of cultural competency that they do now. The idea that everybody, instructors, staff, faculty, and administrators, had to be accountable for people's differences, and respect those differences" (Ragunan, 2016).

Marks says that instructors and administrators who had never served did not consider the difficulty of transitioning from the military to an academic environment. Moreover, veteran students on campus would not readily "self-identify," so their presence was not obvious to many of their instructors or peers (Marks, 2016).

14.2.5 Issue Five:
The Challenge of Fitting in

Brian Ragunan, who served a total of six years in the Marine Corps on active duty and in the reserves, says that military students used to be considered "outliers" who did not fit in with the conventional norms of a college campus. Consequently, they had a difficult time adjusting to the narrow parameters of a curriculum that was almost exclusively geared toward mainstream learners (Ragunan, 2016).

Marks adds that military students just did not have the time to become part of the campus community. Most were married, had children, and worked to support their families. But, he adds that the more investment students make in school, by getting involved in on-campus activities, the better chance they have of succeeding (Marks, 2016).

14.2.6 Issue Six:
Rising Veteran Drop-Out Rate

For those veterans who did decide to venture onto a college campus once they had completed their service, the prospect of success was definitely not guaranteed. A higher percentage were likely to drop out before completing their degrees. Whether the circumstances that led to their unsuccessful attempts to get an education were as a result of the lack of support on campus, or the lack of understanding on the part of their instructors, veteran learners were having a difficult time.

Moreover, veterans were more likely than their civilian counterparts to either attempt or contemplate suicide. Being home again meant too great an adjustment for those who did not know how to make the transition back to the culture of a civilian environment. "In 2005, I saw three young Iraq veterans, back to back to back, try to go to school, only to drop out or flunk out, or get a job, and then try to go back to school again.

"For me, it was like a river of Vietnam veterans," Marks says, referring to the young service members he saw returning from Iraq and Afghanistan. "It was the same . . . story I had heard forty years ago. But, I said to myself: 'Not on my watch; not this time'" (Marks, 2016).

14.3 THE STATE OF MILITARY EDUCATION TODAY

> I am not concerned that you have fallen; I am concerned that you arise.
> –Abraham Lincoln

14.3.1 Progress:
Warrior-Scholar Program: A Step in the Right Direction

Inroads are being made to incorporate the military learner into the classrooms at some of this nation's top colleges and universities. Marla Geha designed the curriculum for science courses that were taught onsite through the Warrior-Scholar Project. (As previously mentioned, Sidney Ellington, who wrote the forward to this book, heads the Warrior-Scholar Project, an organization whose mission is to successfully transition military learners from the battlefield to the classroom.) "The main criteria for admission is the desire for higher education," Geha says. "We are trying to unlock their potential and show them what their options are" (Geha, 2016).

Geha also says that the students who participated in the program at Yale were either active-duty service members who were within a year of transitioning or students who had successfully completed at least one year of community college. A total of fifteen veterans were selected for the "one-week boot camp," based on their motivation and passion to advance their skills.

When Geha first started working with military learners, curricula were only offered in the humanities. But she observed through her own experiences of seeing fewer women pursuing a profession in the sciences, that military students needed similar opportunities. "I do see a lot of commonality between issues that women in science have faced and have talked about a lot, with transitioning veterans students. Issues like 'imposter syndrome,' a lack of mentors, and a general lack of confidence" (Geha, 2016).

At Yale, Warrior-Scholar students attend classes for fifteen hours a day. Geha says that she believes such an intensive schedule is necessary to stimulate learning and establish a strong support system. "I think it is very difficult to create the feeling of teamwork within the academic context, without this kind of intensive schedule."

Geha also contends that the students who complete this program are better consumers of higher education, who know how to apply to schools and how to recognize their opportunities. "Just with my experience in the Warrior-Scholar Project, you cannot teach motivation and drive, you can teach facts and skills. But the unteachable parts are extremely important" (Geha, 2016).

Geha would like to start a fellowship program at Yale so that some of the alumni of the Warrior-Scholar Program will be eligible for hire in the university's research laboratories. To date, she has only received positive feedback from other professors with whom she has shared her idea. "I view the Warrior-Scholar alumni as an extraordinary asset that the science community is losing. And, I think these warrior scholars will change perceptions of veterans from the academic side" (Geha, 2016).

14.3.2 Progress:
New Options: Technology in Learning

The post–9/11 GI Bill was passed about a decade ago. Consequently, the learning platforms that military students had available to them also grew from traditional classroom structures to increased online learning options and a proliferation of for-profit schools.

But Harvard University graduate student Logan Leslie says that veterans who participated in the Iraq or Afghanistan wars are often not as tech savvy as their civilian student counterparts. For instance, these returning service members are not really likely to be consumers of social media.

Leslie cites his own experiences as an example. "Fellow students who were born ten years after I was—after 1986—were likely to be light years ahead of me in technology competency. I owned a computer, but did not really use it very much until I went to college" (Leslie, 2016).

14.3.3 Progress:
Increased Support from the Administration

Curtis Coy says that colleges and universities are beginning to recognize their veteran military students in unique ways. For instance, some campuses across the country have set up veteran centers so student veterans can talk to other individuals who have been or are going through similar transitional experiences.

Coy indicates that among the schools which have taken such steps in the right direction are Arizona State University, which has established the Pat Tillman Veteran Center, and Syracuse University, which created the Institute for Veterans and Military Families. Additionally, some schools, like the University Alabama, have a veteran advocate in each academic department. "When you stand back and look at the 1.6 million folks who are going to school on the GI bill in the past number of years . . . you can see why it's important for schools to adopt efforts to recognize and support the student Veteran population," Coy says. "Schools are now making sure that professors, support staff, and administrators, deans, chancellors, and presidents, have a keen appreciation for veterans" (Coy, 2016).

Coy offers his own anecdotal reference about encouraging veteran recognition when he has been asked to deliver commencement speeches on college campuses across the country. "When I do commencement addresses, I ask all of the student veterans and their parents and families to rise and be recognized. Those family members have endured a lot to support their veteran who is about to graduate from school. I also ask all of the veterans in the audience to stand up and be recognized, because there are a lot of older veterans that deserve recognition as well" (Coy, 2016).

Coy also describes what the VA has done to increase support for student veterans. This includes a program called, "Career Scope," which helps veterans assess their "aptitudes and interests." Additionally, he indicates that the VA has a "GI Bill Comparison Tool" on the GI Bill web site, a streamlined web-based tool that allows veterans and their family members to calculate estimated GI Bill benefits, research certain school attributes, and compare educational institutions.

Coy also mentions that educational centers exist on every military installation, equipped with trained staff members who can offer advice to transitioning service members on academic disciplines and interests, schools, and related departmental programs. And some schools are part of the VA Vet Success on Campus (VSOC) program, which aims to help service members, veterans, and all eligible VA beneficiaries succeed and thrive through a coordinated delivery of on-campus benefits assistance and counseling, leading to completion of their education and preparing them to enter the labor market in viable careers. VSOC counselors provide community and on-campus outreach, communication with VA beneficiaries to address questions regarding VA education benefits, health services, and general VA benefits, as well as educational and career counseling.

As far as the services offered by the colleges themselves, Coy says that more and more schools are establishing veteran service centers, staffed by a faculty member who has military experience. Another resource that Coy recommends is talking to local representatives of the Student Veterans of America chapter (Coy, 2016).

14.3.4 Progress:
Increased Presence of Instructor Support

As an instructor, you do not want to feel you are responsible for singling any student out in front of the class for issues related to his or her background or performance. But if you have ever discussed your concerns about how to approach military students with other instructors, you may have gotten different reactions. You may feel more confused now than when you decided to try and search for some answers.

Logan Leslie says the needs of the enlisted person and the commissioned officer are not the same. He also comments that all undergraduate veteran students were enlisted soldiers, whereas the majority of those enrolled in graduate programs were predominately officers who had to get a bachelor's degree before assuming their previous rank in the military. Leslie speaks from experience, because he completed his undergraduate degree at Harvard College in three years, after eight years of enlisted service, with a 3.76 GPA and is now enrolled in the JD/MBA at Harvard University. He offers educators the following advice:

> I think there are two different ways that professors look at veterans, because there are two different types of military learners that go to school. Undergraduate veterans have very different needs, because

they were all enlisted and didn't have a college education prior to going into the service. However, the vast majority of graduate students who are military learners are officers (Leslie, 2016).

Curtis Coy believes that veterans are able to almost seamlessly adapt to their new surroundings with the right support. Their goal is to complete a mission, which begins with passing a course, completing a degree, and finally, finding a job in the community. "What we see is that veterans who attend school are more likely to be serious about what they are doing. Quite frankly, they have been taught to adapt and adjust, depending upon the circumstance" (Coy, 2016).

But in this process of adapting, veterans may have to learn to reach out for help, if needed. Although that may run counter to their military training, where seeking support could be perceived as a sign of weakness, Coy says the transition is both logical and doable. "They are people who easily mentor and lead others" (Coy, 2016). And he suggests that you can augment these leadership abilities in group activities by assigning a veteran to each one. "Ninety percent of the time, the veteran will take a leadership role, and those students will quickly learn what being a veteran is all about" (Coy, 2016).

But Leslie maintains that most enlisted service members are approaching the educational process without any idea of what to expect once they enroll in school.

> There are really no military resources at all to mentor enlisted soldiers to think about what schools they should attend. And furthermore, there is an institutional disdain for enlisted soldiers who leave the service to attend school. So enlisted veterans have to figure it out for themselves. On the other hand, officers are already exposed to what opportunities they have waiting for them when they do choose to leave. They are aware of their opportunities, whether it is to attend graduate school, or to start a career (Leslie, 2016).

Leslie's own anecdotal information can help you understand the struggles that sometimes separate the traditional from the nontraditional learner (Figure 14.1).

14.3.5 Progress:
Reduced Presence of False Promises from Private Schools

Even though the intent of such legislative efforts as the post–9/11 GI Bill was to provide more educational benefits for military learners, many students became targets of institutions that made false promises about career options after graduation. In more recent years, however, some of the largest private, for-profit institutions responsible for these unethical practices were forced to close after President Obama added stricter operating guidelines to the 2012 "Executive Order—Establishing Principles of Excellence for Educational Institutions Serving Service Members, Veterans, Spouses, and Other Family Members." The updated rules advised that schools address such issues as occupational placement rates, reduc-

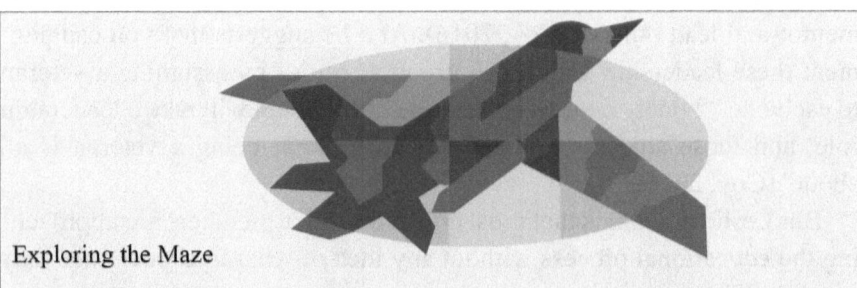

Exploring the Maze

    When I was separating from the Army, I had a brand new baby. I had already applied to schools, but it was going to be a huge challenge for me to make the financials work. My tuition was pretty much taken care of through scholarships and veterans benefits, but I still needed to support my family. It is hard to support your family when you are unemployed. So, because of that, I was concurrently applying to jobs, and in spite of the fact that I had multiple years of combat experience, I was not even getting callbacks from the resumes I sent out to jobs that were not even really that competitive. It was all because I didn't have an education.
    So, I think educators need to know that when they have an undergraduate veteran, he is likely to be in the same situation. I was already on the path to separating from the service, but because I didn't have a good job as a fallback, I was going down a road toward getting a degree, and there was no turning back.
    Essentially, I had been supporting myself for my whole adult life, and I remember the first week of college we had just put down my daughter, and I was studying on my bed. I looked over at the light on the night table, and immediately wondered how I was going to be able to do this for four years, because there was no money coming in (Leslie, 2016).

Figure 14.1. Exploring the Maze.

ing overwhelming educational loan debt, and offering reliable information on cost-benefit returns (Obama Administration Announces Final Rules to Protect Students from Poor-Performing Career College Programs, 2014).

14.3.6 Progress:
Ivy League Acceptance

Depending on which expert you ask, you may get a completely different opinion about the sensitivity of Ivy League schools toward military learners. But Curtis Coy approaches the low enrollment numbers from a positive perspective. First, he maintains that the actual acceptance rate among a more broad-based nationwide applicant pool is actually quite low, so the enrollment figures for veterans just makes sense.

"I was at Columbia University, which is considered one of the pedigree schools on the East Coast," Coy says. "We went around the table and each of the veterans indicated how they ended up at Columbia. One reoccurring theme was that they considered getting in to be a challenge they would meet, even though they had doubts about being accepted" (Coy, 2016).

14.3.7 Obstacle:
Ivy League Presence

If you teach at one of these country's top institutions, you may notice that military learners are not a strong visible force in your classroom. But are you aware of why this situation exists?

According to Logan Leslie, institutions are interested in recruiting these students, but many do not apply. What he believes is that, regardless of whether military learners plan their college education while they are still enlisted, they should still be made aware of what their opportunities are. This information needs to be given to them while they are still in the service, and the message must include input from private-industry employers as well. "They need to hear it from their command, and they need to hear it from industry that they are not going to be able to achieve what they are capable of achieving without an education" (Leslie, 2016).

But he also believes that elite institutions like Harvard and other Ivy League schools should do more to reach out to prospective military students. "Harvard has 6,700 students and two undergraduate veterans, which is unacceptable. I think you would be hard-pressed to find two of any other subset of learners in this nation's top colleges. Furthermore, I have interacted with the admissions department a great deal, and they all want veterans in the institution" (Leslie, 2016).

14.3.8 Information from the "Harvard White Papers"

Harvard banned ROTC recruiting on campus for forty-two years. But President Faust removed that restriction in 2011 for all service division programs, with the exception of the Air Force ROTC. Statistically, the number of military students enrolled since the ban was limited is almost negligible. However as of 2015, only two veterans were enrolled in Harvard College, which is the learning arts division of the oldest learning institution in the country. And Harvard University is among only a handful of colleges in the country that do not provide credit for most ROTC-required courses. According to a 2014 survey of 6,700 Harvard College undergraduates at Harvard College, "44% believe that Harvard does not support the military" (Spain & Fisher, 2015).

Trevor Pontifex believes that the academic standards at these top-ranked schools are quite different from the military's requirements.

> You do not have to be a strong reader or writer to succeed in the military. We do take some correspondence courses, but they tend to focus on military-specific topics, such as terrorism awareness, and small-unit leadership classes. These courses are very basic; especially the ones that just require you to read a book, and take a test on your own.

He also does not hold the institution necessarily responsible for the lower enrollment numbers.

> "Some people are just not going to turn into scholars overnight. Such a task would be beyond the scope of colleges and universities." Using his own experiences at Pomona College to explain his point of view, Pontifex said, "I wouldn't expect this college to accept just any veteran and believe that they could mold that individual into a high-performing student" (Pontifex, 2016).

On the other hand, Logan Leslie believes that the military learners are just not applying in large numbers to the nation's top schools. What he advises is for the colleges to do a better job by spending some money to hire new admissions officers. These school representatives can go and talk to veterans where they are, and that is on military bases. Harvard does not have anyone who goes to the military bases.

> The wars in Iraq and Afghanistan have been the number-one foreign policy issue for 15 years now, and it has changed the course of this country, and to not have individuals with first-hand experience represented in the study body is a great disserve to the institution. Harvard could definitely be doing more to reach out to veterans. It is not as a favor to the veterans, but an effort to achieve a more diverse student body (Leslie, 2016).

14.3.9 Obstacle:
Clear Policies on the Value of Transfer Credits

> There are two educations. One should teach us how to make a living and the other how to live.
> –President John Adams

Another topic discussed in this text is whether military credits are given the same transfer value as community college or university credits during the admission process. Some military courses are not perceived as having the same academic rigor as classes completed at public or private postsecondary schools.

Curtis Coy suggests that, "[i]t would be very challenging to legislate schools to accept another school's credits. Some are very liberal and some are not. I know of schools that do not accept any credits, period. I know one Ivy League school that does not accept another Ivy League school's credits. What we tell people is 'know before you go'" (Coy, 2016).

But Alexander Baldwin McCoy states that it is not possible to lump all the training classes and workshops offered by the military under the same umbrella. Some of these courses are extremely rigorous and should definitely be eligible for transfer credits. McCoy says that recent changes in the review process have allowed applicants to submit a portfolio of their work and include a written narrative describing how their military experiences meet the requirements for a specific class. These portfolios are then evaluated by the institution and, if approved, allow military students to receive full credit.

But McCoy also says that he views this evaluation process as somewhat of a "backward approach," because what service members learn and how they learn can produce different outcomes than instruction that is provided in a civilian classroom. "The push to do transfer credit evaluations of military training runs the risk of portraying training as the equivalent of the civilian version, when it is not absolutely overlapping," he says. "My personal opinion is that we ought to simply accredit more military training itself, rather than try to do equivalency evaluations after the fact," McCoy adds (2016).

14.4 PROSPECTS FOR THE FUTURE OF MILITARY EDUCATION

> As we express our gratitude, we must never forget that the highest appreciation is not to utter words, but to live by them.
> –John F. Kennedy

14.4.1 Goal: Realistic Assessments of Education

According to Joyce Wessel Raezer (2016),

> Over the last decade, I think we have really seen this explosion of education offerings, and some military learners have been overwhelmed by the number of choices they have. The same issues exist for all learners, which is how do I know that the institution is going to provide me with a quality education, and how do I know what a quality education looks like?

Because the federal government crackdown on many private, profit-making institutions, the future will provide answers about establishing a metric for measuring quality education standards.

Further, Wessel Raezer says,

> I think in the future there will be more and more demand for some meaningful regulations or meaningful evaluations of education quality

for everybody. I think the motivator might continue to come from the military side, because of the amount of money that comes from the Post-09/11 GI Bill. So, I think there is going to be demand for the government to pursue quality measurement standards. I also think the smart educational institutions are going to figure out ways on their own to highlight the quality education they provide (Wessel Raezer, 2016).

14.4.2 Goal:
Matching Learning Outcomes to Job Potential

When new veterans enroll in school, what is the best way to establish transferability of credits, so that they are able to get their education and return to the workforce in the timeframe of their civilian peers? Wessel Raezer said such assessments have yet to be made.

She says that another issue that still needs to be addressed is how to match learners' needs to their academic potential. Some military learners are still not making the right choices and paying way too much for an education that could land them minimal career opportunities or earning potential. "Just like the eighteen-year-old who just graduated from high school, some of them do not know what to do. They go to college, but they do not know what to study, or really know what their goal will be. They get their degree and really do not know what to do with it," Wessel Raezer says (2016).

14.4.3 Goal:
Creating Stronger Support Systems before Entering the Academic Environment

Wessel Raezer says that a new step in the transition process is necessary, where an agency or private individual is able to assist service members with matching their skills and experiences with the application requirements for specific schools. She says that the military really does not have an effective program in place to provide this type of advice, although she says that their efforts are increasing in accordance with the downsizing of troop numbers. Issues that need to be discussed during these training sessions include entering school at a much later stage in life than the traditional learner. And because military students have been away from either an educational environment or the workforce for a considerable length of time, another issue that needs to be addressed is how such gaps will affect students' long-term earning potential.

Wessel Raezer says that the issue of providing such training could help the military reduce its financial expenditures of more than $1 billion that has been dispensed to veterans for unemployment compensation over the past several years. This same strategy would apply to vocational skills as well, because a veteran can have spent many months on the battlefield attending sick and wounded service members but also be unable to become certified as an emergency medical technician (EMT) once they leave the service.

Wessel Raezer's advice is to establish a table that allows veterans to list their military schools on one side and be able to compare that information with the metric that these schools use to determine who is eligible for certification. And she says that the VA is already starting to develop programs that will make military education requirements compatible with a civilian certification in some of medical fields.

She also notes that the educational institutions have to exercise a greater level of flexibility, in terms of the courses they accept for college credits. "Some colleges have to be smart enough to say, so we lose out a bit on some of these courses, but we get this person to pay for other courses," she says (Wessel Raezer, 2016). But there has to be someone in the school who is willing to take on this kind of a challenge.

Wessel Raezer adds that the ranks of service members is dove-tailing off as the military gets smaller, so she is not sure how visible these learners will be on college campuses within the coming decade. Moreover, she says that the rush to apply GI Bill benefits to academic pursuits will probably be decreasing as well. But, she says, military learners will also be present, and for institutions that provide education to these students, there is an opportunity to offer higher degrees to adult learners who have a greater interest in expanding their knowledge. Perhaps, too, the issue of being overcharged for an education will not be as much of a problem, if the government continues to move in the direction of making the first two years of college a free option for everyone.

Other issues that could impact military learners' education future include the handling of the student loan crisis. "And, even if the military continues to downsize its ranks," Wessel Raezer says, "these learners will remain present at colleges and universities across the country" (Wessel Raezer, 2016).

So, she adds, "I think there is an obligation that I would hope these institutions take seriously, not just to take military learners' money, but to welcome them, and to celebrate the life experience they bring to that institution, as well as to include them in their outreach. This is always going to be a unique learning population" (Wessel Raezer, 2016).

14.4.4 Goals for the Academic Institution

Curtis Coy indicates that the challenge of making sure that instructors are aware of the needs of military learners starts at the top. What he advises is that schools incorporate an orientation segment for faculty into their hiring practices. To support his idea, he describes such a practice that has been instituted at the University of Alabama, where a retired colonel serving as the director of Veteran Student Affairs is responsible for student and faculty orientations. If a pattern for successful programs exists, we should bring in the directors of veterans' support services at campuses across the country and have them share and exchange ideas. "You raise awareness one step at a time" (Coy, 2016).

14.4.5 Goal for Instructors

Now as you reach the end of this handbook, try to decide how to approach your military learners. Have you come to any concrete conclusions? Maybe not. But hopefully, you have enough information to know that these students have served our country and deserve to have their expectations met in an academic environment. You are not expected to have all of the answers, and you may still have at least a few more questions you would like to have answered. But keep in mind that this handbook is intended as a guide, and the final decisions of which experts' opinions to follow or which approach mentioned more closely mirrors your own pedagogical approach, is really up to you.

But please note the final advice given to you by Logan Leslie, who believes the best instructional approach for establishing a strong, working relationship with your military students is to treat them with respect, but to see them as normal people who are in your classroom to learn. "I think instructors should have agnosticism toward the military learner; it helps to normalize the learning environment. Generally speaking in class, treating vets like a normal student will help them integrate into classroom" (Leslie, 2016).

He adds, "For a vet, going to school is not just an education, it is a transition back to the civilian world. It is used to gain perspective on some very extraordinary experiences, as well as to gain prospective on where you want to go and how you are going to get there. And that includes making a social transition" (Leslie, 2016).

So, if you choose to follow Leslie's advice, you will not highlight or single out your military students by asking them to describe their time in the service. But he advises, if you work with them on feeling like part of the class, they will begin to feel less alienated.

> I think it is tremendously helpful to try and make veterans feel normal. Their military experiences are so intertwined with their identities, that if they are not helped to reintegrate back into civilian society, it could really hurt them because I think there is an aversion to hiring someone who is very, very military. An employee wants to hire someone based upon a specific set of qualifications, and they want to hire people they view as normal.

Trevor Pontifex adds that one of the best resources an instructor can offer to military students is just to speak to them directly and make them feel welcome. He says that this advice extends to letting students know the instructor is available to assist during regular office hours or after class, and that the instructor has time to listen when the student feels like talking. But Pontifex also suggests that pressing military learners for details about their experiences is not a good idea. "The military part of my life is hard to share. I will hear something that reminds me of these experiences, and it immediately changes the nature of the conversation. At a certain point, the conversation dries up" (Pontifex, 2016).

Leslie adds,

> I also think that for the 18-year-old student who is in a class with a military learner, he or she could feel a little alienated from another student that is older, and especially if that student is wearing the military identity on his or her sleeve. And I don't blame that 18-year-old for feeling that way. For most veterans, I think it's a constant struggle to learn to be more approachable.

SELECTED REFERENCES

"10 Things to Consider When Joining the Marines." (2016). Retrieved from About Careers: http://usmilitary.about.com/od/marinejoin/a/choosemarine.htm.

"§1087vv. Definitions." (n.d.). Retrieved from Office of the Law Revision Counsel United States Code: http://uscode.house.gov/search.xhtml?searchString=Homeless&pageNumber=1&itemsPerPage=100&sortField=CODE_ORDER&action=search&q=SG9tZWxlc3M%3D%7C%3A%3A%3A%3A%3A%3A%3A%3Afalse%3A%7C%3A%3A%3A%3A%3A%3A%3A%3Afalse%3A%7Cfalse%7C%5B%3A%3A%3A%3A%3A%3A%3Afalse%3.

"About Military OneSource." (2016). Retrieved from Military OneSource: http://www.militaryonesource.mil/education-and-employment/higher-education-for-service-members.

"Air Force Core Missions." (n.d.). Retrieved from Global Vigilance, Global Reach: http://www.af.mil/Portals/1/documents/newGV_GR_GP_PRINT.pdf.

"Air Force Personnel Demographics." (2016, March 31). The Official Web Site of the Air Force Personnel Center. Retrieved from: http://www.afpc.af.mil/library/airforcepersonneldemographics.asp.

American Council on Education. (2016). Retrieved from "College Credit for Military Service: Transfer Guide: Transfer Credit Checklist": http://www.acenet.edu/news-room/Pages/Transfer-Guide-Credit-Checklist.aspx.

"Answers to the Top Marine Corps Questions." (n.d.). Retrieved from Military.com: http://www.military.com/join-armed-forces/marine-corps-recruiting-faqs.html#pilotmc.

Barnes, J. R. (2015, November 1). "A Military Veteran's Perspective on Integrating into College." Retrieved from 2015 GSA Annual Meeting in Baltimore, Maryland, USA (1–4 November, 2015), Geological Society of America Abstracts with Programs. Vol. 47, no. 7, p. 48: https://gsa.confex.com/gsa/2015AM/webprogram/Paper264846.html.

Braun, L. C. (2015). "Communication & Understanding: Perceptions of U.S. Navy Women with Abnormal Cervical Cancer Screening & Follow-up Care." Retrieved from Uniformed Services University of the Health Sciences: https://www.usuhs.edu/tsnrp/presentation-abstract/communication-understanding-perceptions-us-navy-women-abnormal-0.

Buzzell, C. (2011, September 30). "Johnny Get Your Textbook." Retrieved from Vantage Point: Official Blog of the U.S. Department of Veterans Affairs: http://www.blogs.va.gov/VAntage/4866/johnny-get-your-textbook/.

Callahan, R., & Jarrat, D. (2014). "Helping Student Service Members and Veterans Succeed." *Change: The Magazine of Higher Learning* 46, no. 2, pp. 36–41.

Chickering, A. W., & Gamson, Z. F. (1987, March). "Seven Principles For Good Practice in Undergraduate." Retrieved January 12, 2016, from Washington Center News: http://www.lonestar.edu/multimedia/SevenPrinciples.pdf.

Chrisinger, D. (2016, March 3). Associate lecturer, College of Letters and Science, University of Wisconsin–Stevens Point. Personal interview (S. L. Bricker, interviewer).

Chrisinger, D., ed. (2005). *See Me For Who I Am : Student Veterans' Stories of War and Coming Home*. Albany: Hudson Whitman Excelsior College Press.

Clayton, R. (March 23, 2012. Last updated: February 5, 2015). University of Redlands: "The Military Wallet." Retrieved from 10 Reasons to Join the Military: http://themilitarywallet.com/reasons-to-join-the-military/.

Clever, M., & D. R. Segal. (2013). "The Demographics of Mlitary Children and Families." *Future of Children*, vol. 23, no. 2. Retrieved September 9, 2016, from https://www.fcd-us.org/assets/2014/08/Chapter201.pdf.

"Coast Guard History: Frequently Asked Questions." (2016, June 13). Retrieved from United States Coast Guard, U.S. Department of Homeland Security: http://www.uscg.mil/history/faqs/celeb.asp.

CollegeAtlas.org. (2015, July 16). Retrieved from The Benefits of a College Degree: http://www.collegeatlas.org/earn-a-college-degree.html.

Comerford, M. T. (2011, March 30). "Women change Navy roles through effort, dedication." Retrieved from *The Flagship*: http://www.militarynews.com/norfolk-navy-flagship/news/navy_history/women-change-navy-roles-through-effort-dedication/article_9a2223c7-0ce3-5051-8e21-435ed74a5d3b.html.

Coy, C. L. (2016, November 4). Deputy undersecretary for economic opportunity, Department of Veterans Affairs. Personal interview (S. L. Bricker, interviewer).

Cronin, J. (2016, April 5). Vice president of UMUC's Stateside Military Operations. Personal interview (S. L. Bricker, interviewer).

"Design and Teach a Course." (n.d). Retrieved March 1, 2017, from Carnegie Mellon, Eblery Center Teaching Excellence & Educational Innovation: https://www.cmu.edu/teaching/designteach/design/yourstudents.html.

DiDesidero, D. L. (2016, October 5). Director of the Leadership Communications Skills Center at Marine Corps University, in Quantico, VA. Personal interview (S. L. Bricker, interviewer).

Douglas-Gabriel, D. (2016, June 1). "What Trump University Has In Common With Another For-Profit College." *Washington Post*. Retrieved from: https://www.washingtonpost.com/news/grade-point/wp/2016/06/01/what-trump-university-has-in-common-with-another-failed-for-profit-college/.

Dreon, O. (2013, May 13). "Faculty Focus: Higher Ed Teaching Strategies From Magna Publications." Retrieved from Tips for Building Social Presence in Your Online Class: http://www.facultyfocus.com/articles/online-education/tips-for-building-social-presence-in-your-online-class/.

Ellington, S. T. (2016, January 20). Executive director, Operation Opportunity Foundation, The Warrior-Scholar Project. Personal interview (S. L. Bricker, interviewer).

Elliott, M., Gonzalez, C., & Larsen B. (2011). "U.S. Military Veterans Transition to College: Combat, PTSD, and Alienation on Campus." *Journal of Student Affairs Research and Practice*. Retrieved March 1, 2017, from http://www.tandfonline.com/doi/abs/10.2202/1949-6605.6293

Ermold, J. (2013). *Military Cultural Competence Online Course*. Retrieved from RC (Reserve Component) Challenges: http://www.essentiallearning.net/student/content/sections/Lectora/MilitaryCultureCompetence/index.html.

"Fact Sheet: Veteran Homelessness—Questions and Answers on Homelessness Policy and Research." (2015, April 22). Retrieved from Natoinal Alliance to End Homelessness: http://www.endhomelessness.org/library/entry/fact-sheet-veteran-homelessness.

Fanella, D. P. (2016, April 21). Instructor designer, DDE-ISG, U.S. Army War College. Personal interview (S. L. Bricker, interviewer).

"FAQ About Homeless Veterans." (n.d.). National Coalition for Homeless Veterans. Retrieved from: http://nchv.org/index.php/news/media/background_and_statistics/#faq.

Flaherty, C. (2014, March 20). "Writing instructors consider issues they face when teaching veterans." Retrieved from Inside Higher Education: https://www.insidehighered.com/print/news/2014/03/20/writing-instructor.

SELECTED REFERENCES

"Glossary of Career Education Programs." (n.d.). Retrieved from Study.com: http://study.com/articles/Become_a_US_Marine_Education_and_Career_Roadmap.html.

GoArmy.com. (n.d.). Retrieved from U.S. Army: http://www.goarmy.com/.

Golden, K. (2015, January 15). Deputy director, government relations, Military Officers Association of America (MOAA). Personal interview (S. L. Bricker, interviewer).

Hayek, C. T. (2011, June). "A Nonexperimental Study Examining Online Military Learner Satisfaction and Retention." Dissertation submitted to Northcentral University Graduate Faculty of the School of Education. (ProQuest). Retrieved December 03, 2015, from http://search.proquest.com.ezproxy.umuc.edu/docview/894251223.

Haynie, D. (2013, May 7). "Veterans Weigh Pros, Cons of Online Education." *U.S. News & World Report: Education.*

"Help Center." (n.d.). Retrieved from USAJobs, an official site of the U.S. Government: https://www.usajobs.gov/Help/working-in-government/unique-hiring-paths/veterans/.

"Here's why most Americans can't join the military". (2015, Sept. 26). Retrieved from Business Insider - Military and Defense: http://www.businessinsider.com/heres-why-most-americans-cant-join-the-military-2015-9.

Hinds, C. S. (2016, February 12). "Research Review on Traumatic Brain Injury, Irritability and Aggression." Retrieved October 13, 2016, from http://dvbic.dcoe.mil/files/DVBIC_Research_Research-Review_TBI-Irritability-Agression_Feb2016_v1.0_2016-04-05.pdf.

"Homeless Veterans Facts." (n.d.). National Coalition for Homeless Veterans. Retrieved from: http://nchv.org/index.php/news/media/background_and_statistics/#facts.

Horton, A. (2011, September 28). "At War: Notes From the Front Lines." Retrieved from *From Solider to Student: A Bumpy Road*: http://atwar.blogs.nytimes.com/2011/09/28/from-soldier-to-student-a-bumpy-road/.

Howell, T. (n.d.). "Fact #1. You have 10–15 Years to Use Your GI Benefits." Military.com. Retrieved from: http://www.military.com/education/gi-bill/5-must-know-gi-bill-facts.html.

Hunter, T. (2014, August 25). "The Three Worst Myths About Veterans That Need National Debunking." Retrieved from http://www.takepart.com/article/2014/08/25/veteran-op-ed.

Irving, D. (2016, June 26). *"The Resilience of Military Families."* The Rand Review. Retrieved from: https://www.rand.org/blog/rand-review/2016/06/the-resilience-of-military-families.html.

"Jobs after the Military." (2016). Retrieved from Military-school-source.com - University Bound: http://military-school-source.com/jobs-after-military.aspx.

Kness, R. & M. O'Neill. (2016). "Higher Education Resources for Veterans and Their Families: More than 150 resources to help student veterans and their families overcome the challenges of higher education and career training." Retrieved May 28, 2016, from Community for Accredited Online Schools: http://www.accreditedschoolsonline.org/resources/higher-education-for-military-veterans/.

Lagan, C. (2014, February 5). "From the Homefront: Top 10 things we wish people knew about Coast Guard life." Retrieved from Coast Guard All Hands: http://allhands.coastguard.dodlive.mil/2014/02/05/from-the-homefront-top-10-things-we-wish-people-knew-about-coast-guard-life/.

Lederman, J. (2016, June 2). "Obama warns Air Force grads not to succumb to isolationism." *AirForce Times*. Retrieved from: http://www.airforcetimes.com/story/military/2016/06/02/2016-air-force-academy-graduation/85293418/.

Leslie, L. (2016, October 7). Army Special Forces veteran. Personal interview (S. L. Bricker, interviewer).

Lighthall, A. (n.d.). "Ten Things You Should Know About Today's Student Veteran." Retrieved from National Education Foundation: http://www.nea.org/home/53407.htm.

Lindholm, J. S. (2005, September). "The American College Teacher: National Norms for the 2004-2005 HERI Faculty Survey." Retrieved from Higher Education Research Institute, University of California, Los Angeles: http://heri.ucla.edu/pr-display.php?prQry=25.

Martin, T. S. (2014, August 29). "Understanding Military Culture." Retrieved March 1, 2017, from http://bamaatwork.com/2014/08/29/understanding-military-culture/.

SELECTED REFERENCES

Massi, A. (2014, May 23). "US Army Is Most Respected Branch Of US Military, But the US Navy Is One Of the Least Respected." *International Business Times.* Retrieved from: http://www.ibtimes.com/us-army-most-respected-branch-us-military-us-navy-one-least-respected-1589457.

McBain, L. Y. (2012, July). "From Soldier to Student II; Assessing Campus Programs." Retrieved December 24, 2015, from http://www.acenet.edu/news-room/Documents/From-Soldier-to-Student-II-Assessing-Campus-Programs.pdf.

McCann, C. (2014, March 24). "Million Records Project Explores Student Veterans' Outcomes." *New America.* Retrieved from: https://www.newamerica.org/education-policy/edcentral/million-records-project-explores-student-veterans-outcomes/.

MacDermid Wadsworth, S. (2016, August 31). Director of the Military Family Research Institute at Purdue University. Personal interview (S. L. Bricker, interviewer).

McCoy, A. B. (2016, June 04). Political science student at Columbia University and former Marine Sergeant. Personal interview (S. L. Bricker, interviewer).

"Mental Health Effects of Serving in Afghanistan and Iraq." (2015, August 13). Retrieved from PTSD: National Center for PTSD - Public: This section is for Veterans, General Public, Family & Friends: http://www.ptsd.va.gov/public/PTSD-overview/reintegration/overview-mental-health-effects.asp.

"Mental Health Services: Common Challenges & How to Help - Common Challenges During Readjustment." (n.d.). Retrieved from VA Health Care: http://www.mentalhealth.va.gov/communityproviders/docs/readjustment.pdf.

"Message From CASF." (n.d.). Retrieved from Global Vigilance, Global Reach: http://www.af.mil/Portals/1/documents/newGV_GR_GP_PRINT.pdf.

n.a. (n.d.). "Mild TBI Symptoms." Retrieved from Traumatic Brain Injury.com: http://www.traumaticbraininjury.com/symptoms-of-tbi/mild-tbi-symptoms/.

"Military Students and Veterans." (2016). Retrieved from American Council on Education: http://www.acenet.edu/higher-education/Pages/Military-Students-and-Veterans.aspx.

Miscik, C. (2016, July 22). Air Force tech sergeant—E6. Personal interview (S. L. Bricker, interviewer).

Mitchell, K. (2016, April). "Understanding Academic Reasonable Accomodations for Post-9/11 Veterans with Psychiatric Diagnoses, Part 1: The Foundation." *Federal Practioner.* Retrieved from: http://www.mdedge.com/fedprac/article/107864/mental-health/understanding-academic-reasonable-accommodations-post-911.

Mixon, J. (2014, January 28). "14 common misconceptions about the military: Veterans sort the truths from the myths." Retrieved from Military 1: https://www.military1.com/army/article/404369-14-common-misconceptions-about-the-military/.

Molina, D., & A. Morse. (2015). "Military-Connected Undergraduates: Exploring Differences Between National Guard, Reserve, Active Duty, and Veterans in Higher Education." Retrieved from: https://www.naspa.org/rpi/reports/military-connected-undergraduates-exploring-differences.

Mulrine, A. (2015, November 11). "For many vets college is scarier than Afghanistan." *Christian Science Monitor.* Retrieved from CSMonitor.com: http://www.csmonitor.com/USA/Military/2015/1111/Veterans-Day-For-many-vets-college-is-scarier-than-Afghanistan.

Myers, M.. (2015, October 30). "Navy to expand spots for sailors to take 3 years off." *Navy Times.* Retrieved from: http://www.navytimes.com/story/military/careers/navy/2015/05/31/navy-career-intermission-expansion-coming-soon-congress/28033943/.

The NASPA Research and Policy Institute, in partnership with Inside Track. (2013). "Measuring the Success of Student Veterans and Active Duty Military Student." Retrieved from: https://www.naspa.org/images/uploads/main/NASPA_vets_13%281%29.pdf.

National Center for Education Statistics. (2016). "Characteristics of Postsecondary Students." Retrieved March 1, 2017, from The Condition of Education; Letter From the Commissioner; U.S. Department of Education Institute of Education Sciences: http://nces.ed.gov/programs/coe/indicator_csb.asp.

National Conference of State Legislatures, a. c. (2016). "Veterans and College." Retrieved from National Conference of State Legislatures: http://www.ncsl.org/research/education/veterans-and-college.aspx

SELECTED REFERENCES

"Navy Celebrates 2016 Women's History Month." (2015, September 17). Retrieved from America's Navy: Official Site of the U.S. Navy: http://www.navy.mil/submit/display.asp?story_id=93362.

"Navy Skills for Life." (n.d.). Retrieved from America's Navy: https://www.navy.com/navy-skills-for-life.html.

New York Civil Liberties Union. (n.d.). Military Myths. Project on Military Recruitment and Students' Rights. Retrieved January 17, 2016, from http://www.nyclu.org/milrec/myths.

Obama, B. (2012, April 27). "Executive Order—Establishing Principles of Excellence for Educational Institutions Serving Service Members, Veterans, Spouses, and Other Family Members." Retrieved April 21, 2016, from The White House, Office of the Secretary: https://www.whitehouse.gov/the-press-office/2012/04/27/executive-order-establishing-principles-excellence-educational-instituti.

n.a. (2014, October 30). "Obama Administration Announces Final Rules to Protect Students from Poor-Performing Career College Programs." Retrieved from U.S. Department of Education: http://www.ed.gov/news/press-releases/obama-administration-announces-final-rules-protect-students-poor-performing-career-college-programs.

OWL: Purdue Online Writing Lab. Retrieved from: https://owl.english.purdue.edu/owl/.

Pontifex, T. (2016, September 16). Pomona College geology major, and former Marine sargeant. Personal interview (S. L. Bricker, interviewer).

Prah, C. R. (2014, April 24). "What Exactly Is a 'Military-Friendly' School?" Retrieved from U.S. Department of Veterans Affairs: http://www.blogs.va.gov/VAntage/13871/what-exactly-is-a-military-friendly-school/.

Ricks, T. (2012, May 2). "Voice: Liberal academic joins Navy reserve, students & puzzles several faculty colleagues." Retrieved from Foreign Policy: http://foreignpolicy.com/2012/05/02/liberal-academic-joins-navy-reserve-stuns-puzzles-several-faculty-colleagues/

Romano, L. (n.d.). "4 Simple Strategies to Help a Shy Student." Retrieved from Teach HUB.com: K-12 News, Lessons & Shared Resources: http://www.teachhub.com/4-simple-strategies-help-shy-student.

Roost, A. R. (2014, May–June). "Supporting Veterans in the Classroom: Veterans bring unique challenges that require a focused faculty response." Retrieved from AAUP: American Association of University Professors: http://www.aaup.org/article/supporting-veterans-classroom#.Vungk-aUIXE.

Rue, R. E. Sr. Captain, U.S. Army. (2015, January 11). Personal interview (S. L. Bricker, interviewer).

Saathoff-Wells, T., A. Dombro, K. Blaisure, A. Pereira, & S. MacDermid Wadsworth. (2016). "Teaching about military families: Lessons from the field." Retrieved from National Council on Family Relations Report Magazine, Family Focus Articles, Military Families: https://www.ncfr.org/ncfr-report/focus/military-families/teaching-about.

Sales, D. K. (2015, January 24). "Suicide, Veterans, and PTSD." Retrieved from PTSD Update: http://www.ptsdupdate.com/suicide-veterans-ptsd/.

Schuck, E. (2012, May 2). "Voice: Liberal academic joins Navy reserve, stuns & puzzles several faculty colleagues." Retrieved from Foreign Policy: http://foreignpolicy.com/2012/05/02/liberal-academic-joins-navy-reserve-stuns-puzzles-several-faculty-colleagues/.

Shaw, J. (2015, June 17). "10 Statistics You Didn't Know About Veteran Homelessness." Retrieved from Newsmax.com: http://www.newsmax.com/FastFeatures/homeless-veterans-statistics/2015/06/17/id/651049/.

Sloane, W. (2013, November 11). "Annual Veterans Count, 2013." Retrieved from Inside Higher Ed: https://www.insidehighered.com/views/2013/11/11/number-veterans-enrolled-elite-colleges-drops-essay.

Sloane, W. (2015, November 11). "Where Are the Veteran Students, 2015?" Retrieved from Inside Higher Ed: https://www.insidehighered.com/views/2015/11/11/where-are-veterans-elite-colleges-and-not-essay.

Smith, S. (2016, June 10). "Things to Consider When Deciding Whether to Join The Navy." Retrieved from About Careers: http://usmilitary.about.com/od/navyjoin/a/choosenavy.htm.

Smucny, D., & M. Stover. (2013, March). "Enhancing teaching and learning for active-duty military students." *American Sociological Association: ASA Footnotes,* 41 (3).

Spain, E. S. P., & D. T. Fisher. (2015, May 25). "The Long Crimson Line: White Paper on the Integration of Harvard University and the Military." Retrieved from http://www.advocatesforrotc.org/harvard/2015WhitePaper.pdf.

Starr-Glass, D. (2013, September). "Experiences with Military Online Learners Toward a Mindful Practice." Retrieved December 3, 2015, from *Merlot Journal of Online Learning and Teaching*: http://jolt.merlot.org/vol9no3/starr-glass_0913.htm.

Statistics, P. b. (2016, May). "Department of Veterans Affairs: Statistics at a Glance." Retrieved from United States Department of Veterans Affairs: http://www.va.gov/vetdata/docs/Quickfacts/Homepage_slideshow_06_04_16.pdf

Statistics, P. b. (2016, March). "Profile of Veterans: 2014 - Data from the American Community Survey." Retrieved from United States Department of Veterans Affairs: http://www.va.gov/vetdata/docs/SpecialReports/Profile_of_Veterans_2014.pdf

Stewart, A. (2016). "SVA Chapter Voices—University of Alaska, Anchorage." Retrieved from Student Veterans of American: http://studentveterans.org/35-media-news/latest-news-2014/200-sva-releases-findings-from-the-million-records-project.

Stilwell, B. (2015, September 28). "Here's why most Americans can't join the military." Business Insider: Military and Defense. Retrieved from http://www.businessinsider.com/heres-why-most-americans-cant-join-the-military-2015-9.

"Students Lack Interest or Motivation." (n.d.) Retrieved from Carnegie Mellon: Eberly Center: Teaching Excellence and Educational Motivation: http://www.cmu.edu/teaching/solveproblem/strat-lackmotivation/lackmotivation-04.html.

Sweizer, J. (n.d.). "Accomodations for Active Duty Military Students: What are the federal regulations concerning the treatment of military distance learning students?" WCET: Connect; Learn; Advance. Retrieved from: http://wcet.wiche.edu/wcet/docs/q-and-a/WCETQA-ActiveDutyStudents.pdf.

Szoldra, P. (2013, February 7). "14 Things You Should Know About Enlisting In The US Marines." Business Insider: Military and Defense: http://www.businessinsider.com/things-to-know-before-enlisting-marines-2013-2.

"TBI Basics." (2016, September 9). Retrieved from Defense and Veterans Brain Injury Center: http://dvbic.dcoe.mil/about-traumatic-brain-injury/article/tbi-basics.

Thiem, T. (2016, April 21). Strategic planner, Office of the Assistant to the Joint Chiefs of Staff for National Guard and Reserve Matters, Pentagon. Personal interview (S. L. Bricker, interviewer).

The Tongue and Quill. Retrieved from: http://static.e-publishing.af.mil/production/1/saf_cio_a6/publication/afh33-337/afh33-337.pdf.

"Types of Military Service." (n.d.). Produced by the U.S. Department of Defense. Retrieved from Myfuture.com: http://www.myfuture.com/military/articles-advice/types-of-military-service.

"UMUC at a Glance." (2015, October 16). Retrieved from Global Media Center: http://www.umuc.edu/visitors/about/ipra/glance.cfm.

"A United States Coast Guard Life and Services Handbook: Sea Legs." (n.d.). Retrieved from "The Family Member's Guide to the U.S. Coast Guard": http://www.dcms.uscg.mil/Portals/10/CG-1/cg111/docs/sealegs/sealegs.pdf.

"The Unique Role of the U.S. Coast Guard." (2016). Retrieved from Military.com: http://www.military.com/join-armed-forces/coast-guard-mission-values.html.

VA Campus Toolbook Handout. (2012, April 6). Retrieved from Student Veteran Experiences on Campus: http://www.mentalhealth.va.gov/studentveteran/docs/ed_commonadjustment.html.

Vacchi, D. (2013, September 3). "Welcoming Veterans to Campus." Huffington Post Politics Blog. Retrieved January 16, 2016, from: https://www.naspa.org/constituent-groups/posts/welcoming-veterans-to-campus.

Washington University in St. Louis. (2012, June 7). "A strong bond to an idea makes collaboration more challenging." Retrieved from ScienceDaily: www.sciencedaily.com/releases/2012/06/120607142246.htm.

"Welcome to the Community College of the Air Force (CCAF)." (2015, July 10). Retrieved from The Air University: http://www.au.af.mil/au/barnes/ccaf/index.asp.

SELECTED REFERENCES

Wessel Raezer, J. (2016, October 1). Executive director of the National Military Family Association. Personal interview (S. L. Bricker, interviewer).

"What are good reasons for joining the Air Force rather than the Army or the Navy?" (2015, September 14). Retrieved from Quora: https://www.quora.com/What-are-good-reasons-for-joining-the-Air-Force-rather-than-the-Army-or-the-Navy.

The White House—President Barack Obama. (n.d.). "Joining Forces: Education." Retrieved from: https://www.whitehouse.gov/joiningforces/issues/education.

"Who are civilian contractors and what jobs do they perform overseas?" (2016, May 16). Retrieved from POC (Professional Overseas Contractors, LLC): http://www.your-poc.com/what-are-civilian-contractors-and-what-do-they-perform-overseas/.

"WWII in American Music: Pre-War Defense." (2012). History on the Net. Retrieved from: https://search.yahoo.com/yhs/search?p=WWII+in+American+Music%3A+Pre-War+Defense%2C+2012&ei=UTF-8&hspart=mozilla&hsimp=yhs-001.

Zenko, M. (2016, May 18). "Voice: Mercenaries Are the Silent Majority of Obama's Military." Retrieved from ForeignPolicy.com: http://foreignpolicy.com/2016/05/18/private-contractors-are-the-silent-majority-of-obamas-military-mercenaries-iraq-afghanistan/?wp_login_redirect=0.

Zinger, L. (2010, January). "Contemporary Issues In Education Research: Veterans Returning From War Into the Classroom." Retrieved January 3, 2016, from The Clute Institute: http://www.cluteinstitute.com/ojs/index.php/CIER/article/view/160/153.

Zinman, D. A. (2010). "Book Review: *AWOL: The Unexcused Absence of America's Upper Classes from Military Service—and How It Hurts Our Country*, by K. Roth-Douquet & F. Schaeffer." (New York: Harper Collins, 2006). doi:DOI: https://doi.org/10.1177/0095327X09356259.

Zoli, C., R. Maury, & D. Fay. (2015, November). "Missing Perspectives: Servicemembers' Transition from Service to Civilian Life—Data-Driven Research to Enact the Promise of the Post-9/11 GI Bill." Institute for Veterans & Military Families, Syracuse University.

INDEX

Absent Without Leave (AWOL), 34
Acknowledgments *(this book)*, xv–xvi
active-duty learner, 102
Air Force: airmen, 82; distinguishing features, 81. *See also* Community College of the Air Force (CCAF)
Adams, John, quote from, 137
Alcott, Louisa May, 76
All-Volunteer Force (AVF), 77
American Council on Education (ACE), 9, 45, 91; *See also College Credit for Military Service* (ACE Website link); Defense Activity for Non-Traditional Education Support (DANTES); U.S. Department of Defense
Army: commissioned officers, 68; warrant officers, 67
Army War College, 58

Brown University, 9
building credibility, 17
Business Insider (magazine), 77, 109
Buzzell, Colby, 5; blog post, 5

campus resources, 18
Carnegie Mellon University, 42
cell phone use, 13
Center for Preventive Action at the Council on Foreign Relations, 100. *See also* Zenko, Micah (senior fellow, Center for Preventative Action at the Council on Foreign Relations)
Chesterton, G. K. (English writer, poet, and philosopher), 28
Chickering, A. W. and Gamson, Z. F. ("Seven Principles for Good Practice in Undergraduate"), 13, 23
Chrisinger, David, 46. *See also See Me For Who I Am*
Churchill, Winston, 101
civilian contractor, 100
Coast Guard, 100; Coast Guard Reserves, 87; Coast Guard Auxiliary, 87; "Coasties," 87; duties, 88; rescue swimmers, 88
College Credit for Military Service (ACE Web site link), 49–68
common myths, 23
Community College of the Air Force (CCAF), 82. *See also* Air Force
Cronin, James, 44
Coy, Curtis L., 124, 132, 133, 135, 138, 141

Dartmouth University, 9
Date Eligible to Return from Overseas (DEROS), 34
Defense Activity for Non-Traditional Education Support (DANTES), 48; DANTES Information Bulletin (DIB), 50
deployment: definition of, 66

Dewey, John, quote from, 13
Dickens, Charles, 113
DiDesidero, Linda (director of the Leadership Communications Skills Center at Marine Corps University), 119–121. *See also* Marine Corps University
distance education, 53
Duke University, 9

Einstein, Albert, quote from, 99
Eisenhower, President Dwight D., quote from, 61
Ellington, Sidney, 32. *See also* Foreword *(this book)*; Warrior-Scholar Project

Emerson, Ralph Waldo, quote from, 118

Family Educational Rights and Privacy Act (FERPA), 120
Fanella, Daniel (instructional systems specialist for the U.S. Army War College's Department of Distance Education), 5, 57–59
Flaherty, Colleeen, 41
Foreignpolicy.com, 77. *See also* Schuck, Eric
Foreword *(this book)*, ix–xii
for-profit schools, 126
Franklin, Benjamin, quote from, 41

Geha, Marla (professor of astronomy and physics at Yale University), 124, 130
Gen. MacArthur, Douglas, quote from, 109
GoArmy.com, 67
Golden, Karen (deputy director of government relations for MOAA), 56
grading policies, 38
Gulf War, 110

Harris, Kamala (California Attorney General), 95
Howard, Michelle (four-star Navy general), 76
Horton, Alex (public affairs specialist at the Department of Veterans Affairs), 55

The International Business Times (newspaper), 75

Internet café. *See* "morale welfare and recreation" (MWR)

Johns Hopkins University, 9

Keller, Helen, quote from, 9
Kennedy, John F., 138

Leslie, Logan (U.S. Army Special Forces Veteran, now serving in the Special Forces of the National Guard and attending the JD/MBA program at Harvard University), 125, 130, 133, 135, 137, 142
LGBTQ community, 32
Lighthall, Alison ("Ten Things You Should Know About Today's Student Veteran"), 11, 12, 67
Lincoln, Abraham, quote from, 129

McCoy, Sergeant Alexander (political science student at Columbia and former Marine), 62, 124, 126; *New York Times* Op-Ed piece, 19
Marks, Michael William (professor of practice in psychology; director, Supportive Education for Returning Veterans–SUMCVETS Center, University of Arizona), 124, 126, 128
Marine Corp University, 119
Marines: description of, 71; conditions of enlistment, 72
military culture, 6, 17, 19, 22, 26, 31, 37
military documents, 36. *See also* plagiarism
military-friendly: curriculum, 33; blog by Capt. Robert Prah, 48. *See also* U.S. Department of Veteran Affairs web site
military learner, 3; defined, 7; same as military student, xiv; "nontraditional" students, 2; goals, 16
military sexual trauma (MST), 111
military student, xiv; classroom observations, 12; goals, 4, 16; "nontraditional" students, 2; same as military learner, 3
military withdrawals, 45
Miscik, Candice (Air Force reservist), 83

INDEX

Mitchell, Katherine L. (former medical director, Phoenix VA Medical Center Post-Deployment Clinic; current specialty care medicine lead for the Veterans Integrated Service Network Office 22), 113, 114
Molière, quote from, 19
"morale welfare and recreation" (MWR), 54

NASPA–Student Affairs Administrators in Higher Education, 25, 26, 69
National Coalition for the Homeless, 68; veteran statistics, 68
National Conference of State Legislatures, 6, 24, 68, 69
Navy: Basic Underwater Demolition Unit, 77; Career Intermission Program, 79
Navy Reserves. *See* Schuck, Eric
New York Civil Liberties Union, 26
"nontraditional" students, 2; definition, 2; military learner, 3
Northwestern University, 9

Obama, Michelle,, 105
Obama, President Barack, 95; executive order, 59, 134
orders to deploy, 37
The Owl at Purdue, 15

Pat Tillman Veteran Center, 131
plagiarism, 35. *See also* military documents
Pontifex, Trevor (Pomona College geology major and former Marine sergeant), 124, 136
Presley, Elvis, quote from, 32
post–9/11 GI Bill, 4, 20, 44, 59, 66, 94, 110, 130; tuition, 18, 123; medical benefits, 29
posttraumatic stress disorder (PTSD), 9, 30, 38, 111
Princeton University, 9

Ragunan, Brian (program coordinator of vets/services for transfer and reentry students (STARS) at University of California, Santa Cruz), 125, 126, 128, 129

RAND Corporation, 104
reservist. *See* active-duty learner
Ricks, Thomas (Pulitzer Prize–winning journalist), 77
Romano, Loriana, 16
Roosevelt, Eleanor, quote from, 106
Roosevelt, Theodore, quote from, 3
Rue, Captain Robert, 54, 55

Schuck, Eric, 77–78
See Me For Who I Am, 46. *See also* Chrisinger, David
special accommodations : notification of, 18; privacy rights, 19
Stanford University, 9
Starr-Glass, David, 9
Stein, Bill (former Air Force communication officer), 81
Student Veterans of America: Million Records Project, 94. *See also* Veterans Success Club (UMUC)
Sweizer, James, 55
syllabus: instructional elements, 18; academic paper, 32, 34; special accommodations, 18; working contract, 36; practical considerations, 40
Syracuse University's Institute for Veterans and Military Families, 110

team structures: *ScienceDaily*, 22; Flaherty, Colleen, 22
The Tongue and Quill, 34, 110
Thiem, Lt. Col. Terry, 3, 53, 60; deployment schedule, 3
tour of duty, 27
traditional learner, 2; definition, 2; returning learners, 2, 16
traumatic brain injury (TBI), 38, 112, 113, 115
Trump, Donald. *See* Trump University
Trump University, 96
tuition, 18. *See also* post–9/11 GI Bill
Turnitin.com, 35

United States Marine Corps (USMC), 72
University of Chicago, 9
University of Maryland University College (UMUC): campus model, 43; Prior Learning Program, 45

U.S. Army War College, 5
U.S. Bureau of Labor Statistics, 96
U.S. Department of Defense, 6, 48, 49; *Military OneSource*,; TA DECIDE database of schools, 50
U.S. Department of Defense Voluntary Education Partnership Memorandum of Understanding (MOU), 55
U.S. Department of Education, 95
U.S. Department of Educations' National Center for Education Statistics, 66
U.S. Department of the Navy, 72
U.S. Department of Veteran Affairs web site, 50, 60; "School Resources" homepage, 47
U.S. News & World Report : education section, 48; tips from Marine veteran, 48

VA Campus Toolbook, 9, 11, 17, 47, 55; "What Can I Do To Help?" 47; fact sheet on veteran learners, 47
Vacchi, David, 25
VA Vet Success on Campus (VSOC) program, 131

veterans: adjusting to civilian life, 118; definition, 92; chronic physical pain, 118; homelessness, 92; appointments without competition, 96
Veteran's Administration, 95
veteran learner, 17
Veteran's Success Club. *See* Student Veterans of America, 43

Warrior-Scholar Project, 32, 129–130
Washington, George, quote from, 75
Washington University, 9
Wessel Raezer, Joyce (executive director of the National Military Family Association), 104, 106, 124, 141

Yale University, 9
Yeats, William Butler, 42

Zenko, Micah (senior fellow, Center for Preventative Action at the Council on Foreign Relations), 100
Zinman, Donald A., 62

ABOUT THE AUTHOR

Suzane L. Bricker is an associate adjunct online professor at the University of Maryland University College (UMUC), and a peer editor for the *Journal of Business and Technical Communication* (JBTC).

www.ingramcontent.com/pod-product-compliance
Lightning Source LLC
Chambersburg PA
CBHW020740230426
43665CB00009B/502